PRIVATE GARDENS OF
PARIS

PRIVATE GARDENS OF

PARIS

MADISON COX

PHOTOGRAPHY BY PHILIPPE PERDEREAU

HARMONY BOOKS
New York

Illustrations:

JACKET FRONT: M. Yves Brieux-Ustaritz's formal box parterre, *IXe arrondissement.*
JACKET BACK: scented country courtyard in the *V^e arrondissement.*

HALF-TITLE: a striking white statue stands at the head of the box and gravel parterre.

TITLE: *Left*, in a corner of M. and Mme Landolt's garden, a black marble statue is surrounded by vivid tulips in spring.
Right, a shady outdoor dining area in the Landolts' garden.

INTRODUCTION: *Right*, colourful plantings of tulips, roses and daffodils characterize Mme Dauchez's garden.
Left, tables and chairs placed under the shade of climbing roses add a country-garden feel to this heavily scented garden.

Published in the United States of America by Harmony Books, a division of Crown Publishers, Inc.,
225 Park Avenue South, New York, New York 10003
Published in Great Britain by George Weidenfeld & Nicolson Limited
HARMONY and colophon are trademarks of Crown Publishers, Inc.
Manufactured in Italy

Library of Congress Cataloging-in-Publication Data
Cox, Madison
Private Gardens of Paris/by Madison Cox:
photographs by Philippe Perdereau.
224 p.   cm.
1. Gardens—France—Paris.   2. Gardens—France—Paris—Pictorial
works.   3. Paris (France)—Description—1975-   I. Perdereau,
Philippe
II. Title
SB466.F8C69 1989
712'.6'094436—dc19   89–1749
ISBN 0–517–57336–9   CIP
10 9 8 7 6 5 4 3 2 1
First American Edition

Designer Ruth Hope

CONTENTS

INTRODUCTION

City gardens are endowed with a unique feature: whatever their shape or size, and whatever their design, they are all retreats from the hubbub of city life, places where one can sit undisturbed and forget the bustling crowds and traffic. Other than this – indeed, perhaps because of it – they are as individual as their creators, reflecting personal tastes and preferences, needs and purposes. Dotted all over Paris, the gardens described here demonstrate to the full the extraordinary variety of styles, made all the more memorable when contrasted with the public face of a city that is familiar to all.

Above all, however, the gardens are not only reflections of personal taste, they are thriving tributes to the care with which they are tended. Cities – and Paris is no exception – are notorious for their disadvantageous growing conditions: poor soil, insufficient light and polluted air. Yet every one of these gardens flourishes thanks to the patience and expertise of those who look after them. Moreover, they are full of an enormous range of plants, displayed to their best advantage; an inspiration to all city dwellers struggling with their own retreat.

This success comes partly from regular tending and partly from a definite, carefully considered pre-planting scheme. Such a scheme may consider many factors; horticultural and personal, historical and aesthetic. Some have been devised by the owners themselves, others by renowned garden designers; some result in luxuriant, profusely planted 'country' gardens, others in elegant, classically symmetrical expanses re-creating the great gardens of seventeenth-century France. Whatever their style, all are practical, stimulating, and inimitably French.

I

A RURAL COURTYARD

Mme Gallia Saouma
XIVe arrondissement

Paris is full of carefully nurtured gardens, not only the broad green expanses of the *VIIe arrondissement* or the lush, picturesque gardens of the *XVIe*, but also the hundreds of tiny plots scattered all over the city. They lie behind carved stone façades and high brick walls, wedged in angles between tall buildings and squeezed into the most unpromising spaces. As the city's tree-lined boulevards and shady parks and squares provide its public counterbalance to the congested urban environment, so these small plots are Parisians' private response. Highly individual and as diverse in character as the people who created them, they are for private enjoyment rather than for public show.

Nowhere are there so many of these tiny gardens as in the outlying *arrondissements*. Gallia Saouma's diminutive plot, bordering the city's southern perimeter, is a colourful and very personal garden created with the help of her friend (the landscape gardener) Jacques Valdi.

This small five-by-eight-metre space in the furthest reaches of the *XIVe arrondissement* backs on to a unique feature

Previous page left, the summer planting scheme devised by Mme Saouma and Jacques Valdi replaces the vivid pinks, blues and whites of the spring growths with more restful shades of green and white.

Previous page right, a carved sea creature adds a whimsical touch as it emerges from tumbling honeysuckle, *Lonicera fragrantissima*, planted along the garden wall.

Right, a weeping beech shades Mme Saouma's collection of vivid red-flowering rhododendrons and azaleas, its leaves adding further splashes of colour and form to this densely planted garden.

of the Parisian landscape, the wooded banks of the *petite ceinture* – the old railway. Constructed in the mid-nineteenth century to circle the city, the line is now abandoned except for short stretches of its north-western section. The narrow strip of land behind Mme Saouma's house and garden has sprouted a dense covering of woodland which acts as both a backdrop and a borrowed landscape of dappled shade to extend the horizons of the tiny garden.

Wedged between the steep wooded bank and a stone party wall, the rectangular garden is shielded from the Rue Beaunier by high railings. As the garden was designed to be viewed from inside the house, most of its colour was concentrated in a bed overlooked by the large glass doors that give access to it. Some seventeenth-century terracotta tiles found on the site were embedded in the narrow earth and gravel path between house and garden in order to break up the unplanted surface, and a number of rocks, carefully chosen for their strange or unusual shapes,

were used by M. Valdi to edge the flowerbed.

While it enjoys uninterrupted exposure to the sun during the spring, in summer the south-facing site is cast into deep shade by the dense foliage of the neighbouring trees, so Mme Saouma planned the planting accordingly: 'Given the limitations of the site I finally decided on lots of bright colour in spring, with crocuses and tulips, giving way in summer to shade-loving plants which would create a totally different kind of atmosphere.'

In early spring there are masses of purple and white *Crocus imperati*, followed by drifts of vivid yellow and white tulips, including the lady tulip, *T. clusiana*. A native of the northern mountains of Afghanistan, it was found by M. Valdi and added to the bed, where its pointed white petals splashed with red made an unusual sight. Blocks of strong colour are provided by dozens of hyacinths including masses of the Roman hyacinth, *H. orientalis* 'albulus', which produce up to twenty stalks of small flowers. Perfume is provided not only by the spring bulbs but also by carpets of old-fashioned stocks, currently in shades of white, cream and blue, though the colour scheme is always evolving. 'I used all different colours and tones in the bed, which of course have to be supplemented every few years,' says M. Valdi. Twisting overhead, along the far wall, is a winter honeysuckle, *Lonicera fragrantissima*, which bears heavily fragrant white flowers in April.

In devising the planting scheme with M. Valdi, Mme Saouma wanted to re-create her childhood memories of the lush growth and opulent colours and scents of the southern Mediterranean. As many of the plants she remembered so fondly would never have survived in her garden, she chose a collection which would remind her, directly or obliquely, of her old Mediterranean favourites. 'The garden is really based more on cultural associations and on similarities of colour or shape than on any attempt to create a real Mediterranean garden, which would have been impossible. As we couldn't plant bougainvillea, for instance, one of my favourites for its rich colour and exuberant growth, Jacques and I trained bright red-flowering roses over the metal fence. The image they create, though different, is every bit as strong as the one I remember.' They also planted large double-flowered camellias which, while they survived (they have since succumbed to a series of hard frosts), carried with them all the luxurious connotations of the Far East and Japan.

While the possibilities for using tall shrubs were obviously limited by the size of the site, M. Valdi did employ a few flowering evergreens in the far corner. Near the shade of a weeping birch he planted velvety, red-flowering azaleas, the small leaves of evergreen *Rhododendron indicum* contrasting with the large foliage of an 'Essex Scarlet' rhododendron, also chosen for its deep crimson flowers.

As the summer goes by so the garden takes on ever softer colour schemes. Groups of irises add touches of deep blue and purple, echoed by the tall, delicate blue spikes of campanula. Masses of greater celandines, *Chelidonium majus* begin to spread everywhere, engulfing the beds with their deeply serrated leaves and buttercup-yellow flowers which bloom throughout the summer. Another plant that brought back memories for Mme Saouma was the Algerian scarlet flax, *Linum grandiflorum* 'Rubrum', which they eventually found after much trouble. Sown in early spring this hardy annual fills odd corners with the touches of red that for Mme Saouma symbolize summer and the passing of time. Weaving in among the winter honeysuckle is *Lonicera* x *herckrottii*, which bears cascades of fragrant pink flowers with bright golden stamens in summer. Along the back wall the buds of large clumps of Japanese anemones, *A. hupehensis*, rise on slender stems, ready to bloom in late August. The summer planting scheme, which flowers until the first heavy frost, carries with it the air

of soft languor which goes with the lazy heat of July and August.

In this cramped space, full of colour and scent, Gallia Saouma and Jacques Valdi have amply demonstrated that a garden does not have to be large or full of a botanical array of plant varieties to be lively and interesting, and that, above all, it is essential in a small space to work with its limitations rather than against them. City gardening, after all, is the art of the possible – which, when practised with skill and tact, as here, can seem almost to achieve the impossible.

The graceful line of tall trees that stands at one end of Gallia Saouma's small garden creates a leafy backdrop that casts a welcome dappled shade in summer.

2

A LUSH
COUNTRY GARDEN

M. and Mme Roger Thérond
XVIᵉ arrondissement

Off the Rue Raffet, in the secluded depths of the *XVIᵉ arrondissement*, a narrow path leads through a tunnel of greenery towards M. and Mme Roger Thérond's secret garden, the sense of mystery heightening with every step. A massive wooden door, silver with age and half-concealed by festoons of climbing roses and a tangled mass of other climbers, guards the entrance to this delightful garden, set a few metres back from the steeply sloping street, and bordering the site of one of the most celebrated gardens in the old village of Auteuil.

When, as late as January 1860, Paris assumed its modern form and was divided into twenty *arrondissements*, the village or *commune* of Auteuil ceased to exist as an autonomous community and was incorporated with three others in the *XVIᵉ arrondissement*. Mentioned in documents going back to the early Middle Ages, Auteuil formerly swept down from the Bois de Boulogne in the north to the banks of the Seine in the south. By the eighteenth century, the green slopes of Auteuil and of the adjacent *commune* of Passy had become a

Above, the yellow blossoms of *R.* 'Elegance'.

Opposite, forsythia and cherry trees smother the unique Norman wing.

Previous page left, the creeper-covered house façade.

Previous page right, a terracotta bust is just one of the garden's numerous hidden surprises.

fashionably rustic setting for the country residences of Parisian notables, who set about creating their own versions of the pastoral idyll then in vogue. One of the most celebrated of these bucolic fantasies, on the present-day site of the Villa Montmorency in Auteuil, was the brainchild of the Comtesse de Bouffler. One of the great *femmes d'esprit* of the late eighteenth century, rival to Madame du Deffrand and Mademoiselle de Lespinasse and mistress to the Prince de Conti, the Comtesse de Bouffler held her brilliant literary *salon* at the Palais de Temple, the Prince's Parisian residence. There she entertained a formidable array of writers and artists, statesmen and philosophers, including Rousseau, Mozart, Voltaire, Madame de Staël and Horace Walpole, a company whose conversation was believed

to be as glittering as its combined reputation. On the Prince's death in 1776 the Comtesse retired, with her daughter-in-law and her *salon*, to her house in Auteuil.

Behind the high walls of the estate she created a *jardin à l'anglaise* of rolling expanses of closely mown fields, carefully placed copses and serpentine walks. Said to have been designed by an English gardener, this carefully ordered 'natural' landscape was entirely in keeping with contemporary notions of gardening, imported from across the Channel and adopted and developed by a number of the Comtesse de Bouffler's intimates, notably Rousseau, who challenged man's domination over the natural world and instead advocated a return to nature.

Within a little over a decade the Revolution saw the Comtesse's downfall, and her estate given over to a series of tenants. These included Talleyrand, who replaced the sweeping lawns – which according to Walpole rivalled the best to be found in English gardens – with wheat, planted in a patriotic gesture more symbolic than fruitful. By 1822 the estate had been acquired by the Duchesse de Montmorency, in whose family it remained until 1852, when the land was cleared and divided up into smaller plots. The part known today as the Villa Montmorency is made up of houses built in the richly eclectic style of the late nineteenth century. The Théronds' garden, situated on the perimeter of what was the Comtesse de Bouffler's estate, still retains something of the secluded, pastoral aura of its eighteenth-century heyday.

From the front door a cool terracotta-tiled passage leads through to the six hundred-square-metre garden, filled with plants growing in profusion and in seemingly careless abandon. Climbers scramble up the half-timbered and ochre-washed house walls, only to cascade down again, laden with blooms. Below, evergreen and flowering shrubs spill over a peaceful patch of lawn, and subtle combinations of rare and tender

The country-garden atmosphere of the plantings is appreciated most fully when the courtyard and the façades are seen from the top of the house.

plants flourish in protected corners. Bursting with life and vivid colour, it is at the same time a place of cool shade and quiet seclusion, of hidden corners and veiled depths that entice the visitor to exploration and discovery.

The core of the Théronds' rambling house is a modest early eighteenth-century building, which stood on the site before the Comtesse de Boufller created her estate, and which in time was reached via a passage in the garden's far corner, now walled up. The house was enlarged over the centuries, until at the turn of the century both house and garden met their match in the American sculptor and art-lover Herbert Haseltine. He enhanced their rustic atmosphere by adding wrought-iron balconies, doors from country houses and antique hanging lanterns. But the most extraordinary structural change came when he added to the side of the house an authentic Norman half-timbered seventeenth-century house. Haseltine discovered it in a large pile in a shop in Rouen, completely dismantled and numbered piece by piece. He bought it, transported it in crates back to Paris, and assembled it in the garden's far corner, linking it to the original

house with an enclosed gallery at first-floor level, and creating a timbered loggia underneath.

The Norman house, with its bulging walls and steeply pitched slate roof, has the same irresistible charm as the rustic pavilions that became such popular features in late eighteenth-century gardens. Marie Antoinette's hamlet in the park behind the Petit Trianon at Versailles is perhaps the most famous – and the most extreme – example. Clustered picturesquely around an artificial lake, it included a Norman farm, a dairy, a windmill and numerous little huts, which for the Queen and her intimates summed up the simple pleasures of rural life, where cows were milked into Sèvres porcelain pails by titled ladies dressed as peasants. Before this, in 1775, the Prince de Condé had built a hamlet at Chantilly with kitchens, a mill and a billiard hall disguised behind Norman half-timbered façades and thatched roofs. As time passed these bucolic whims multiplied, to include the Swiss village at Franconville and the seashell pavilion at Rambouillet, and they became wildly eclectic in style, with, for instance, Tuscan orders supporting thatched roofs. Half-timbered houses, however, became the *sine qua non* of these rustic utopias, and the same romantic notions dictated that gardens should be filled with a tangled profusion of plants. Thus the Théronds possessed all the prerequisites for an atmosphere of positively shameless romanticism.

A curtain of Virginia creeper clings to the house walls, creating a leafy backdrop for the romantic abandon of the rest of the garden's planting. Left to its own devices, this rampant climber spreads in all directions, racing up the walls, round the balcony rails, over the windowsills, along the guttering and across the roofs to the chimneypots. By April it breaks into leaf: feathery pale green in spring, dense mid-green in summer and dazzling scarlet in autumn.

To create an even more extravagant

Virginia creeper frames views from every window in the house.

The garden's far boundary wall is whitewashed annually to offset the magnificent pink-flowering cherry trees and the large-leaved evergreens planted underneath.

The dense, twisted growth of *Philadelphus coronaris* provides a shady canopy for outdoor dining.

Below, glowing a deep crimson in autumn Virginia creeper completely conceals the eighteenth-century ochre-washed façade of the house.

effect, Mme Thérond planted climbing roses which now scramble up the Virginia creeper, using its branches for support. The velvety red blooms of *R.* 'Etoile de Hollande', borne on long, arching canes, contrast with the green leafy walls and patches of ochre façade and add a note of rich colour to the garden

and trained so that it overhangs the terrace, creating a cool area for summer dining. Opposite it a *Choisya ternata* adds its own heady orange blossom perfume.

Framing the views from the salon with their lacy evergreen foliage are stands of bamboo, *Bambusa multiplex*, planted in a narrow bed under the wall, and behind there rises a three-metre-high *Magnolia grandiflora*. Its waxy dark leaves provide part of the garden's evergreen structure. Near the magnolia, which bears large, creamy-white fragrant flowers in late summer, is a mound of vivid yellow forsythia, *F.* x *intermedia* 'Spectabilis', which brings the garden to life in mid-March.

At the bottom of the rectangular lawn, framing a stone terrace and table and against the whitewashed backdrop of a neighbouring wall, are two pink-flowering cherry trees, *Prunus serrulata* 'Kanzan', with a purple-flowering rhododendron beneath. Planted against the white wall are low, large-leaved evergreen shrubs, including *Fatsia japonica*, which make strong silhouettes when seen from the house and create a sense of greater depth.

In another shady corner of the garden, protected by one of the walls of the Villa Montmorency, is a recently planted hollow square of camellias. The raised stone platform is a peaceful retreat from which, in late afternoon light, some of the best views of the garden and house are to be had.

Even in midwinter the garden is full of interest, though most of its dense blanket of foliage has fallen. A twisting tracery of branches covers the walls and roofs, casting swirling abstract shadows on the grey stone terrace below, while the cascading branches of a weeping pear tree, *Pyrus salicifolia* 'Pendula', rise from a mound of glossy evergreen foliage.

In the Théronds' garden, at every season, fantasy and reality combine to create an enchantingly pretty garden which, real as it is, nevertheless seems too pretty to be true.

Opposite, growing among the Virginia creeper the deep pink blossoms of the climbing rose 'Etoile de'Hollande' surround doors and balconies with colour and heady perfume.

while scenting the stone-paved terrace below. Meanwhile, from the top of the timber gallery cascades of *R.* 'Elegance' billow down over the loggia area, the large double yellow blooms seeming to float in mid-air, catching and holding the summer light.

Shading a corner of the house is a towering canopy of mock orange, *Philadelphus coronarius*, which in late June fills the air with the intoxicating scent of its white flowers. Over the years it has been pruned

3

A FORMAL
BOX PARTERRE

M. Yves Brieux-Ustaritz
IXᵉ arrondissement

Yves Brieux-Ustaritz's garden, the quintessence of the baroque embroidered parterre, reflects his passion for seventeenth-century design, coupled with his own flair for theatrical touches. It lies in the middle of the *quartier* Saint-Georges, off the busy Place Pigalle in the *IXᵉ arrondissement*, peacefully hidden behind the early nineteenth-century façades of the Rue de la Rochefoucauld. From the dance studio on the top floor of his late nineteenth-century house, the distinguished dancer can look down on a perfectly symmetrical composition of evergreen rococo arabesques and scrolls, which lies virtually unchanged throughout the year.

The Saint-Georges area, on the lower southern slopes of Montmartre, was developed in the northern expansion of the city during the first half of the nineteenth century and, like Montmartre itself, quickly became home to a community of artists, writers, musicians and actors, who lived cheek-by-jowl with each other and with the many theatres and music halls that sprang up. Further down the Rue de la Rochefoucauld is another typical nineteenth-

century house and attic studio, where Gustave Moreau lived and worked. On his death in 1898 Moreau bequeathed his house to the state, and it is now one of Paris's most charming and least visited museums, containing the largest single collection of the artist's work. Among other artists whose *ateliers* were dotted up and down the street were Millet, John Lewis Brown and Renoir; Victor Hugo also lived here, as did the composers Charles Gounod and Jacques Halevy, whose work *La Juive* inaugurated Charles Garnier's Opéra in 1875.

Unlike many other Paris *arrondissements*, where lush greenery escaping over walls and glimpsed through gates is a clue to the number of gardens flourishing behind the stone façades, the *IXe arrondissement*, and especially the *quartier* Saint-Georges, is not generally associated with private gardens. Yet hidden among the maze of streets that thread their way up and down the district's hills are numerous tiny pockets of green that have somehow managed to survive in this densely built-up area.

One of the finest is undoubtedly M. Brieux-Ustaritz's garden; hidden away at the far end of a series of courtyards behind the grey-shuttered entrance from the street. It was not always so impresssive, as he is the first to admit: 'When I first saw the empty house in 1952, it was the upstairs studio that caught my eye much more than the scrubby patch of grass which then made up the garden.' The studio which so caught his imagination sat on top of the three-storey detached house, a large square room with a pitched glass roof which had served as a painting studio for the previous tenant. M. Brieux-Ustaritz first concentrated his energies on transforming it into an extraordinary dance studio, where he could also carry out his teaching work with members of the Paris Opéra ballet company. He had the glass-panelled roof removed and replaced with a solid white-painted ceiling, from which he suspended an elaborate chandelier

Left, viewed at ground level the fanciful box design stretches to fill the entire garden.

Previous page left, the formal, restful air of the garden is felt most strongly when the low parterre is viewed against the sheltering, neighbouring trees.

Previous page right, providing a central focal point, a nineteenth-century marble statue gleams amid the ivy.

laden with candles. Large baroque mirrored sconces, which he found in Venice and are now fixed to the pale mauve-painted walls, heighten the theatrical, *fin-de-siècle* atmosphere. Swags of red damask frame an enormous mirror covering an entire wall, and the wide north-facing window which overlooks the garden below. The rich draperies and glimmering surfaces are of an extravagant opulence to match the lavish stage sets and scarlet and gold interiors of the Opéra itself, and they demanded an equally positive design statement for the garden below.

One of M. Brieux-Ustaritz's principal de-

The borders of impatiens are broken only by large clumps of hostas and pink-flowering dahlias.

mands was that the view from the house, and more importantly from the studio, should be interesting throughout the year. Flowerbeds were out of the question as they require too much upkeep and look dead in winter, and grass was discounted as he feels it never looks at its best in urban surroundings. What he needed was something stylized, where the element of design was paramount and which would be satisfying to look at from all angles and at every season: 'It seemed the logical solution to create a box parterre.'

The rectangular site, nine metres by fourteen, lies in front of the house, enclosed on three sides by ivy-covered walls. At one end a pair of black-painted iron gates marks the entrance to the garden, and a narrow stone-paved path runs the length of the space, flanked on one side by one of the ivy-covered party walls and on the garden side by a metre-high clipped privet hedge. In spring this is underplanted with vivid pink, scarlet and white impatiens. At the end of this green corridor the path leads on to a terrace running the width of the garden, from which a flight of white stone steps rises to the house. Here, in the small rectangular space abutting the terrace, on axis with the front door of the house and an existing maple tree, M. Brieux-Ustaritz decided to lay out his embroidered parterre.

Once the area had been cleared, he entrusted the design of the parterre to his friend M. Pourat, who recalls: 'As we had decided on a parterre of clipped box, reminiscent of the great French gardens of the seventeenth century, I started by looking at books and engravings of the period to find a design I could adapt to a small site.'

Following in the tradition of the amateur gardeners and designers of the seventeenth century, M. Pourat consulted contemporary published collections of recommended garden designs, which contained a seemingly infinite variety of schemes for the symmetrical parterres then in vogue. Like architecture pattern books, these influential volumes encouraged the latest fashions to spread like wildfire, and before long the *parterre de broderie* was an indispensable feature in any garden of taste. Its first documented appearance was in Jacques de la Barauderie Boyceau's *Traité du Jardinage selon les raisons de la nature et de l'art*, post-humously printed in Paris in 1638. Boyceau's treatise, which is generally considered to mark the origins of the *jardin à la française*, documented the stylized motifs which were to become popular in the early

seventeenth century. The first signs had appeared thirty years earlier, when Olivier de Serres – the great sixteenth-century agricultural theorist and practitioner – published *Le théâtre d'agriculture et mesnage des champs*. In this he discussed the employment of parterres, or *bouquetiers*, filled with flowers and bordered with scented bushes like lavender, thyme and marjoram, and defined the properties of the ideal parterre as perfect symmetry in the layout, and great variety in the flowering plants. By Boyceau's time, a generation later, the scented bushes had been replaced with evergreen box, and the scroll designs they contained, also in box, were set against different coloured sands and crushed stone.

During the early seventeenth century such parterres became more and more fashionable in every field of the applied arts, inspiring floral motifs on textiles for clothing and upholstery and on objects in every medium, including silver, leather and wood. As the demand for evermore intricate de-

A shady dining area in a corner of the formal garden, the arabesque designs on the white-painted chairs echoing the parterre's traditional design.

Long narrow beds planted with a vibrant collection of impatiens edge both the central parterre and the path beside it.

signs grew, garden designers, artists and craftsmen all began to draw their inspiration from each other. All, likewise, were fascinated by the strange-looking plants now being brought back to France from overseas by merchants and explorers which, with their unfamiliar and sometimes bizarre leaf forms and their fantastic fruit and flowers, injected an element of exoticism into the new designs. Boyceau, meanwhile, as 'gentil-homme ordinaire de la chambre du roi' and 'intendant des jardins' to Louis XIII, with responsibility among other things for the new royal gardens at the Palais du Luxembourg, Versailles and the Tuileries, was particularly well placed to encourage interest in them among wealthy and influential clients.

Another important factor in the development of the French garden design in the seventeenth century, and especially in the rapid growth in popularity of the embroidered parterre, was the remarkable Mollet family, which from the late sixteenth century to the late seventeenth century produced a virtual dynasty of royal gardeners. The founder was Jacques Mollet, who was head gardener to the Duc d'Aumale at Anet before moving on to the Tuileries, leaving his son Claude in charge of the gardens. It was Claude Mollet who made the innovation that was to prove so revolutionary in garden design. Struggling to maintain

the *parterre de broderie* designed by the architect Etienne Dupeyrac, he found that every winter the edging plants succumbed to harsh weather and had to be replaced in spring, which was very costly in materials and labour. His solution was to substitute an evergreen plant that was still a novelty, and not a particularly popular one at that: box. His designs illustrated Olivier de Serres' *Théâtre d'agriculture*, while his own *Théâtre des plans et jardinage*, printed posthumously in 1652, reproduced engravings of designs by his sons, André, Jacques and Noël.

During the course of the century the Mollets' influence spread through France – where they were responsible for the gardens at Versailles, Saint-Germain-en-Laye, Fontainebleau and the Tuileries, among others – to the rest of Europe. In Stockholm in 1651 André Mollet published *Jardin de plaisir*, dedicated to Queen Christina of Sweden, in whose service he was employed as chief gardener from 1648 to 1653. This volume laid out the principles then governing not only classic French garden design but also that of most of the rest of Europe, largely as a result of the initiative and influence of the Mollet family. Conceived as a source-book and work of reference as well as an introduction to the *jardin à la française*, the book contained engravings of grand garden layouts and embroidered parterres, and an accompanying text in Swedish and German as well as French.

These works by the two Mollets, de Serres and Boyceau heralded a new era in garden history. By the end of the seventeenth century (when the last recorded Mollet gardener, Jacques' great-great grandson Armand Claude, was still active) the influence of French garden design was to be seen across Europe, from Hampton Court and Chatsworth in England to Sanssouci in Potsdam, and from Drottningholm in Sweden to Nymphenburg in Bavaria. An essential feature of all these was the embroidered parterre, which reigned supreme until the mid-eighteenth century when, with the advent of naturalistic landscaping, its influence began to wane. They enjoyed a brief and colourful renaissance in the late nineteenth century, when they were planted with exotic subtropical blooms. This century has seen a few short-lived attempts to revive their use, most notably by the landscape designers Henri Duchène and his son Achille in their restoration work in the gardens of Vaux-le-Vicomte and Courances, but on a large scale the style is too labour-intensive to be practical nowadays.

In M. Brieux-Ustaritz's small plot M. Pourat designed a central bed, rectangular with one convex side at the far end from the house, in low dwarf box, *Buxus sempervirens* 'Suffruticosa'. The parterre is bordered with a double row of clipped box containing a narrow strip of glossy ivy, which forms a subtle contrast with the small-leafed box. Within this frame is laid out a symmetrical pattern of scrolls and arabesques, punctuated with small round tufts, all executed in box. The design is highlighted by crushed brick used as ground cover, a reference to the traditional use of coloured minerals – sands and clays as well as crushed brick, coal and even seashells – to enhance the 'broderie'. At the far end, under the maple tree, M. Brieux-Ustaritz has positioned a nineteenth-century marble statue to act as a focal point. The luminous whiteness of the marble is echoed by a narrow path of fine white gravel which encircles the parterre and completes the composition, presenting a fitting, un-changing prospect from the flamboyant studio above.

A corner detail of the parterre which, unlike those of the seventeenth century, contains an ivy filler between the two rows of box.

4

A NORMANDY-STYLE COURTYARD

VIIe arrondissement

Just off the busy Boulevard des Invalides in the *VIIe arrondissement* is one of the most surprising houses in Paris. There is nothing unusual in this area about the cobbled courtyard and the massive *porte-cochère*; but when the great wooden doors swing open they reveal a bucolic scene which at first could be mistaken for a piece of the Normandy countryside transported to the capital. The black-and-white half-timbered manor house has witnessed many famous expatriate Americans including Ernest Hemingway, F. Scott Fitzgerald, Elsa Max-

well. The American colony gave many a *fête champêtre* in the garden, while the house was where Parisian flappers first danced the Charleston. Legend has it that Cole Porter, who used this as his Paris home from 1919 until the early years of the Second World War, kept a cow from Normandy in the garden to complete the rural atmosphere. Surrounded by mature sycamores and lime trees and screened from the neighbouring garden by a tall ivy-covered wall, the L-shaped house and its cottage garden seem to have strayed from the Calvados country of

the Pays d'Auge. In recent years the Swiss-born landscape designer Franz Baecheler has been restoring the garden, constantly adding to the planting and judiciously weeding out, so that it may appear once again as it did in its colourful heyday.

Beyond the *porte-cochère*, in front of the central block of the house, is a large rectangular courtyard, bordered on one side by the garden. Here M. Baecheler has used a variety of evergreen climbers and shrubs, all planted in white raised beds and containers, to create a crisp, fresh feel against the

Below left, the airy foliage of a Japanese maple contrasts with the dark trees behind.

Previous page left, planter boxes add an air of formality to the courtyard.

Previous page right, contrasting leaf forms emphasize the lushness of the plantings.

Above left, spreading ferns and ivy tendrils fill the courtyard's white-painted containers.

Right, a continuous line of pink-flowering impatiens brightens up the dense shrubbery.

Below, the half-timbered house, glimpsed through dense foliage that lines the courtyard, appears to be in the middle of the country rather than in the middle of the city.

weathered granite cobblestones. Virginia creeper, *Parthenocissus tricuspidata,* clambers over the half-timbered façades of the house, its tendrils clipped with a touch of architectural formality, to frame windows and doorways. Rising from one of the circular raised beds is a tall cherry tree, underplanted with trailing ivy and ferns, which dominates the courtyard at every season. In winter its gnarled branches create fantastic shadows; in spring, as the delicate fronds of the ferns open, it is smothered with pink blossom; and in summer and autumn its canopy of leaves casts a cool shade. *Fatsia japonica,* with its large, handsome leaves, variegated euonymus and glossy-leaved ivies planted in the other beds contribute to the overall impression of luxuriant growth.

M. Baecheler's choice of planting here was governed by the light conditions, for while some parts of the garden were exposed to the full force of the sun's rays, others were in complete shade. With his experience of conditions as diverse as Normandy and the Tropics, he decided to brighten up the darkest corners with planting which would concentrate on subtle contrasts in foliage form and texture. He therefore avoided busy associations of different variegated leaf types, or of blue- and yellow-leaved varieties or distracting verticals, like the glowing white trunks of silver birch, for these would create contrasts that were too strong in a limited space. Instead he opted for trees and shrubs of compatible forms and colours, which together would produce subtly harmonious effects.

From the courtyard, a gate in the white picket fence that divides it from the garden gives access to a narrow path, which leads to the wide expanse of grass at the garden's centre. The lawn is bordered on one side by the house and terrace, and on two others by dense trees and shrubbery, which test to the full M. Baecheler's ability to enliven dark corners. The fourth side is the sunniest and runs the length of the courtyard.

At the bottom of the garden, opposite the house, M. Baecheler planted long curving banks of rhododendrons, which add spots of soft colour to views from inside the house. Above them, venerable yews have grown to a great height, their shaggy branches extending horizontally. Further along, an equally aged Chinese wisteria has engulfed not only the house façade but also a neighbouring tree, and now cavorts from the guttering.

Among the shady bank of foliage M. Baecheler included a weeping purple beech, *Fagus sylvatica* 'Purpurea Pendula', and, isolated in front of the bank, a dwarf Japanese maple, *Acer palmatum*. The maple's delicate light green summer foliage seems to illuminate the whole area and adds a touch of exoticism, especially in combination with its underplanting of *Helxine soleirolii*. It also seems to echo in miniature the graceful shape of another weeping beech, *F. sylvatica* 'Tortuosa', the large green leaves of which make a sympathetic background to the maple when seen from the house, while contrasting softly with the purple-leaved variety.

This corner manages to sustain year-round interest with its subtle textures and shades, without allowing any one tree or shrub to disrupt the unity of the composition. In winter the skeletons of the ornamental trees make fascinating patterns, their gnarled branches twisting in a staccato dance, constantly shifting in the changing light. In summer, a wide ribbon of bright pink impatiens and red tobacco plants, *Nicotiana alata*, snake round the edge of the shrubbery which seems to swim in a sea of colour.

A couple of years ago, M. Baecheler was asked to devise a way of introducing more colour and flowers to the garden without disrupting the balance that existed between it and the courtyard. His first move was to erect the white picket fence, at once picking up the architectural features of the courtyard and the rustic elements of the garden, while defining both spaces without inter-rupting the views from one to the other. Then, between the lawn and the fence, he laid out two square plots adjoining each other. He edged both with low borders of lavender, and filled them with a profusion of colourful flowers to create the effect of an

Entry from the formal courtyard to the garden beyond is by way of a rural wicket gate.

A black-painted wrought-iron bench stands underneath cascading rose bushes.

Overlooking the lawn, white-painted chairs and a table stand in the shade of the house.

A white picket fence lined with white planter boxes divides the garden from the courtyard of granite cobblestones and brightens the area on even the greyest of Parisian days.

English cottage garden. In one bed red- and pink-flowering camellias are underplanted with mounds of vivid Mollis azaleas in shades of pink and orange, while the second is filled with roses in pale pink, white, deep yellow, scarlet and crimson, all spilling over the

white-painted fence.

A third, smaller patch on the opposite side of the path, also edged in lavender, was planted with *Pieris*, with golden leaves which seem to hold and reflect the afternoon sun. Variegated ivy complements both the euonymus and the dark, glossy leaves of a standard camellia which rises in one corner. This, together with a clematis that climbs up a trellis against the house wall above, adds height and further colour to the area.

Here it is quite easy to forget the urban life hidden behind the high walls – the roar of the traffic and pavements crowded with people – for this is a garden which is designed, quietly and subtly, to deceive. Every detail, from the emerald-green lawn to the luxuriant growth of trees and simple, colourful flowers combines to conspire against the visitor to convince him that outside the door lie the gently rolling hills of Normandy. Perhaps only the cow is missing.

Left, beds filled with lavender, osmanthus, azaleas and roses brighten the lawn's edge.

5

A ROOFTOP TERRACE

Jennifer Bartlett and Mathieu Carrière
VIe arrondissement

This painter's garden is newly created, but for its owner, the American artist Jennifer Bartlett, it represents an expression of a long-held and deeply-felt passion. On a rooftop high above the Rue Vavin in Montparnasse, she has conceived a series of visual effects to stimulate and inspire her painter's eye, while at the same time challenging and delighting the gardener in her. Her guiding philosophy is not directed towards creating seasonal colour, or year-round interest, or any of the other goals that most gardeners strive for. Instead, her fascination – to which

her collection of containers bears witness – is with the process of growth itself. On this unusually verdant rooftop, as much a laboratory as a garden, change and evolution are the dominant themes, and colours, textures and forms are cultivated in order to create exciting associations and unfamiliar, fleeting combinations.

Perched high among the chimneypots and slate roofs of the *VIe arrondissement*'s Montparnasse quarter, with panoramic views over Paris, the garden looks down on the length of the Rue Vavin, from the Jardin du Luxem-

Above, by late summer all the beds and troughs are full of rampant growth, with celery, dill and fennel competing for space.

Right, adding a fanciful yet formal note among an otherwise natural-looking garden, a bush of mint is clipped carefully into a classical ball shape.

Previous page left, every balcony of the apartment block is bordered with a profusion of colourful growth, the foliage and flowers cascading from one level to the next.

Previous page right, fresh white-painted chairs add further splashes of colour to the plant-filled balcony.

and a new concept in design for urban living – rose up halfway down the street.

The Maison à Gradins was designed by the celebrated architect Henri Sauvage as an attempt to reform the living conditions of urban workers. The extraordinary ziggurat-like structure recedes from the street in a series of stepped levels, culminating in a flat roof-space. Along the front of each of the six storeys Sauvage added cement troughs to contain the greenery that he intended to cascade down over the sleek white ceramic tiles with which he covered the building's street façade. Eighty years on the combination of gleaming tiles and spilling greenery still sets the building apart from the neighbouring grey stone façades. On every level a profusion of flowering shrubs, bamboos and colourful perennials is silhouetted against the pale, reflective background.

When Jennifer Bartlett and her husband Mathieu Carrière moved into the top-floor apartment five years ago, they discovered the scattered remains of the previous tenant's terrace garden, including a prolific 'Reine des Reinettes' apple tree growing beside a lilac tree, and a venerable lavender bush, which over the years had swept over the ledge and now presented only its woody stem, while the neighbours below had all the benefit of its foliage and flowers.

Inside the apartment they removed many of the dividing walls to create fewer, larger rooms that were now flooded with natural light. Unlike so many Paris interiors, where light is filtered through layers of curtains and veils of net or lace, here the large windows are all left uncurtained so as to allow the maximum amount of sunshine to stream in. From the central open-plan living area, tall panes of glass give a view over the Parisian skyline, framed by crisp white walls and, in the foreground, the bright colours of the terrace. The muted tones of the interior – natural pale-coloured woods and monochrome black and white – seem to retreat in the face of the balcony's colourful onslaught.

bourg at the northern end to the site of the famous Café de la Rotonde, once the haunt of local artists and writers including Guillaume Apollinaire, Max Jacob, Picasso, Derain and Vlàminck. Once a country path lined with lime trees, in 1831 the Rue Vavin was cobbled and edged with modest single-storey houses, each with a small garden in front. Then, in 1912–13, an extraordinary edifice –

Off the living room's main seating area, a small two-and-a-half-by-five-metre terrace floored with crazy paving contains an assortment of terracotta pots and troughs planted with flowers which seem to merge into blocks of pure pigment: red roses, yellow pansies, orange nasturtiums. Trained up wires are the tendrils of a honeysuckle, *Lonicera japonica* 'Halliana', which perfumes the air with its flowers of white fading to yellow, intertwined with *Clematis montana* 'Grandiflora', which bears a mass of pink anemone-like flowers in spring. The honeysuckle also weaves along the balcony's metal railing to enclose the outdoor seating area.

In mid-spring Jennifer Bartlett plants out sweet pea and nasturtium seedlings, which by the end of July will engulf the entire space. On the balcony's south side she trains the sweet peas up a trellis of bamboo poles and twine so that in summer, when they are in full flower, they make a sweetly scented hedge of delicate, translucent shades of pink, lavender, blue and white against the fresh green foliage. On the floor, an indoor hydrangea, *H. macrophylla* 'Benelux', and pots of nasturtiums add hot pink and orange tones. Along the balcony's secluded northern side, overlooking the trees of the Jardin du Luxembourg, a deep zinc trough is filled in spring with terracotta pots of roses and bulbs, and in summer with cosmos. Below, smaller pots contain basil and mint, sunshine-yellow day lilies, *Hemerocallis* 'Golden Prize', and clumps of bright yellow and purple pansies.

At one end of the living room a floor-to-ceiling window frames part of the eight-metre-long trough that runs the width of the apartment – it is also overlooked by the large painting studio at the far end. Here, silhouetted against the sky, tall spikes of *Delphinium* 'Blue Tit' bloom in summer among a variety of pink, yellow and carmine-red roses. To achieve ever-changing vivid colour combinations, Ms Bartlett relies on an assortment of annuals: sweet peas,

light blue and mauve love-in-a-mist, *Nigella damascena*, African marigolds, California poppies, *Eschscholzia californica*, and snow-in-summer, *Cerastium tomentosum*, flourish under the well-established lavender and lilac.

Frustrated by the limitations imposed by the narrow fifty-centimetre ledge, which seemed to grow more restrictive with every season that passed, Ms Bartlett, like any keen gardener, began dreaming up ways of creating more planting space. With the help of the landscape designer Pascal Cribier she set about designing a practical and light-weight solution.

In Jennifer Bartlett's studio, among half-finished canvases and plans for future garden projects, normally spread out all over the

Before the creation of the rooftop garden this small balcony adjoining the apartment was the only planting area. Jennifer Bartlett continues to fill it with colourful growth throughout the spring and summer.

floor, is a corner piled high with photographs of gardens that have inspired her on her numerous horticultural trips. Another great source of inspiration is her daily afternoon walk through the Jardin du Luxembourg.

Laid out in 1617 for Marie de Médicis, the vast gardens adjoining the newly constructed Palais du Luxembourg were inspired partly by the Queen's desire to re-create the Boboli Gardens, attached to the Palazzo Pitti in Florence where she was born. Beneath Salomon de Brosse's monumental façade there unfurled a large embroidered parterre, interrupted by an octagonal lake and flanked by groves of mature trees. The park remained relatively unchanged until after the Revolution, when the central axis was extended, and in the mid-nineteenth century a *jardin à l'anglaise* was laid out at the far end. The Second Empire craze for bedding out was an important influence on the garden and remains so to this day. Hidden among the trees are beds filled with purple-leaved castor oil plants, *Ricinus communis* 'Sanguinens' and the spidery blooms of *Cleome hasslerana*. Closer to the Palais, more formal, geometric-shaped beds are edged with silvery santolina enclosing waxy pink begonias and deep red standard fuchsias, with yellow-flowered *Lantana camara* and occasional spikes of Canterbury bells, *Campanula medium*. With their constantly changing planting schemes, the beds are an endless source of fascination for Ms Bartlett.

Using the roof's fixed features as he would trees or stone walls in a country garden, M. Cribier employed the various water tanks, chimneys and light wells as elements with which to define each garden space or room. He designed a series of modular, rectangular troughs in unfinished zinc, which he arranged in different formations to create a sense of variety. To the inside face of the troughs he attached low, inconspicuous black-painted metal safety rails.

While the lower terraces were alive with vivid colour, M. Cribier filled the rooftop

The rampant growth and vivid colours of Jennifer Bartlett's rooftop garden.

with foliage plants, massed to create an impression of lush greenery against the sky, and extended in every plane by plants in terracotta pots to add an extra element to the play of heights and volumes in the small space.

There is a great sense of fun and adventure in the rooftop garden, with plants seemingly hiding behind each other, waiting to be discovered or used in odd or surprising combinations, such as the brimming pots of *Hibiscus syriacus*, with semi-double light blue flowers, underplanted with tufts of grass and *Centaurea montana*. A large, symmetrically positioned bed of lavender, *L. officinalis*, is transformed into a lake of blue when in flower, after which the shrubs are clipped back to uniform mounds of dense silver-grey foliage. Chinese wisterias climb up the whitewashed side wall, their light green foliage making a leafy backdrop for the summer-flowering light blue agapanthus, *A. orientalis*. By late summer the garden is dominated by looming sunflowers, staked against the wind, and planted in the same terracotta pots that in spring contained tulips and narcissi. In a few years *Santolina chamaecyparissus*, cotton lavender, will form a low hedge around one of the troughs which struggles to contain billowing clouds of cosmos, with pink and white flowers dotted among their feathery foliage. In this garden of trial and experimentation new ideas and old favourites are employed in daring combinations, and their progress charted with eager expectation.

In a far corner bed stands a solitary sumach, *Rhus copallina*, a rarity in small gardens because of its invasive habit but planted here in the hope of enjoying its brilliant red autumn colour. Nearby, a pink-flowering lilac brightens the area in late spring.

A zinc trough in a quiet corner contains a colourful tangled mass of cornflowers, *Centaurea cyanus*, and a low wall is covered with a spreading sweet pea vine, which bears pure

Left, rows of chives, salvias, carrots and parsley fill the zinc containers perched on the rooftop, while two terracotta trays are planted with bright nasturtiums that spill over the edge.

Below, when Jennifer Bartlett and Mathieu Carrière discovered the balcony garden it was dominated by an old apple tree and large lavender bushes. These still flourish today, their branches and foliage tumbling over the balcony edge.

white flowers. *Malva alcea*, hollyhock mallows, rise over a metre in this precariously windy spot, holding aloft their spikes of pale pink and white flowers. This peaceful retreat, surrounded by the pastel colours of romantic cottage garden flowers and protected from the wind, has become a favourite spot for summer picnics.

Nearby, a terracotta pot standing alone contains what Ms Bartlett refers to as her contribution to the classical French garden: a topiary sphere of spearmint, regularly clipped to preserve its perfect geometry. Shallow dishes are seeded with nasturtiums which engulf the gravel in late summer in homage to one of Ms Bartlett's favourite references: Monet's garden at Giverny.

A water tank clothed with a passion flower, *Passiflora caerulea*, shades a corner planted with Japanese anemones, which rise in late summer from the silver-grey leaves of *Senecio cineraria*. A small osmanthus adds its sweet scent and contrasting foliage to this cool corner.

Running the length of two groups of troughs that contain the highly productive vegetable garden is a hedge of *Phillyrea angustifolia*. This splendid southern-European evergreen shrub lines the outer edge and is pruned to create a dense protective hedge for the neat rows of parsley, carrots, fennel, celery and basil. Chives provide a touch of purple, while dwarf white daisies add splashes of bright contrast at the far ends. *Clematis texensis* twines along the metal railing, and by late summer is lost in the tidal waves of nasturtiums billowing over the beds. The velvety soft silver-grey foliage of *Stachys byzantia* grows next to rows of mint, while sage sends up its spikes of purple flowers beside the 'Butternut' lettuces and feathery carrot tops.

The profusion of greenery that engulfs this small space is the fruit of Ms Bartlett's many late afternoons spent planting, weeding, watering, dead-heading, thinning and otherwise tending her garden. As the summer

draws to a close and she prepares to return to New York for the winter, last-minute plans and ideas for next year's planting are already taking shape in her mind, to await her return the following spring when her annual act of creation will begin again.

The garden zigzags along the roof edge, its fenced compartments appearing maze-like against the skyline of Montparnasse.

6

A GARDEN IN WHICH TO ENTERTAIN

Yves Saint Laurent
VIIe arrondissement

In late July 1986, while seamstresses were feverishly putting the final touches to Yves Saint Laurent's autumn collection, the couturier's *rive gauche* apartment and garden were being transformed for his fiftieth birthday celebration. On the patch of lawn which, spread with oriental rugs and cushions, had seen many a Sunday afternoon picnic, a huge two-storey yellow-and-white-striped marquee rose from a wooden platform. Garlanded with flowers, it was the highlight of a glittering evening – and it inspired Saint Laurent and Pierre Bergé, his

longtime friend and business partner, to redesign the garden.

'We were completely unimpressed when we walked under the *porte-cochère* and saw before us a bleak, grey courtyard with a nondescript looking six-storey brick building at the far end,' says Bergé of the day he and Saint Laurent first visited the apartment, in a turn-of-the-century building on the Rue de Babylone in the *VIIe arrondissement*. Only when they crossed the threshold did they begin to see the possibilities, and when they discovered the garden their minds

One of a pair of whimsical garden chairs, designed by the artist François-Xavier Lalanne who, over the years, also created a number of animals for Yves Saint Laurent's menagerie, including a flock of sheep and white marble ducks.

One of several classically styled *jardinières* planted with clipped box and placed between the series of French windows to add a formal touch to the marble terrace.

Previous page left, simple metal garden chairs and mosaic-topped tables are arranged formally on the white marble terrace against a backdrop of the semicircular amphitheatre.

Previous page right, viewed from the salon on the first floor, the amphitheatre terrace stretches into the lush greenery of the garden beyond.

were made up. They took the apartment then and there.

The finely detailed art deco interiors were commissioned originally for a wealthy American who was bankrupted in the Wall Street Crash of 1929, only a year after the apartment was completed. Mme Cuttoli, the legendary art patron of the 20s and 30s, took up residence immediately after his departure and lived there for forty years until 1969, when Saint Laurent and Bergé moved in. She lined the walls with works commissioned from her artist friends, including Picasso,

Miro, Braque and Dufy, and Saint Laurent feels, imbued the whole apartment with a creative energy. But above all he was enchanted by the private, enclosed atmosphere of the garden, amid the surrounding openness.

The square plot enjoys an unusually protected position, bordered on three sides by adjacent gardens, with a neighbour's tennis court at the bottom. The boundaries are defined only by low hedges and trellis fences thus creating an illusion of much greater space. Surrounded by trees, shrubs and vistas of greenery, and insulated from any street noise, this garden is a haven of seclusion in the heart of the city.

The first change they made in the garden was to construct a four-metre-wide marble terrace the length of the building's garden façade, its glimmering white surface functioning as a continuation of the white library. Two low tables, inlaid with gold mosaic, surrounded by armchairs with simple wrought-iron frames, designed by Jacques Grange, make this an ideal spot for afternoon tea in fine weather. Most of the twenty-metre-square garden was orginally covered in gravel; planting consisted of a few rather straggly rose bushes, surrounded by a low bank of shrubbery. A clump of *Robinia pseudoacacia*, sycamores and chestnut trees shaded the bottom of the garden. As they grew, so the difficulties of maintaining the front lawn, with which Saint Laurent replaced the gravel, increased. He would never allow the trees to be pruned, preferring the randomly patterned shade cast by their branches to open sunlight, with the result that the grass had to be re-seeded annually. At one point, inspired by a number of visits to the Zen gardens of Kyoto, they considered transforming the area into a Japanese garden, but Saint Laurent was reluctant to lose the lush, jungle-like atmosphere. An alternative idea, which was eventually carried out, was to replace the grass with ground cover of ivy and periwinkles, *Vinca minor*. This too

Growing along the window railings, twisting grape vines add touches of greenery that break the otherwise serene, whitewashed façade.

was doomed to failure, as the two dogs of the household made short work of uprooting the lot.

Inspiration finally came from an unexpected quarter: Saint Laurent's house in Marrakesh. The Villa Oasis, a vision of oriental splendour, stands among the luxuriant planting of the Majorelle gardens. The home in the 1920s of the French painter, Jacques Majorelle, both the house and the gardens were sadly neglected by the early 1980s, when Saint Laurent and Bergé took them over and started to restore them. Now open to the public, the gardens are once again a tropical paradise, filled to overflowing with exotic flowering shrubs and climbing plants, such as daturas, bougainvillea, hibiscus and jasmine, among groves of variegated bam-

boo, date palms and sago palms, *Cyca revoluta*.

They have also become a great source of inspiration to Saint Laurent in his work, so in transforming his Paris garden he decided to try to evoke the same atmosphere of lush exuberance.

No matter what they had tried in the past, the front part of the garden had always been a problem. They began to think that what it lacked was a feature of some sort, and after Saint Laurent's birthday party the solution became obvious. They decided to continue the terrace out into the garden. As soon as the marquee had been dismantled, Bergé called in Jean-François Bodin, the architect responsible for the complex Matisse museum renovations in Nice, and who had already

dramatic focal point. Two low, curved balustrades, each supported by four large travertine globes, define the edge of the area and double as bench seating. Between them, on a stone plinth, stands a seventeenth-century statue of a Minotaur. The man-size creature, one of the many priceless treasures in Saint Laurent's collection, emerging from the tangle of evergreen foliage behind, seems quite in keeping with this classical arena.

Construction work on the raised platform spread chaos and destruction among the plants, so Franz Baecheler, the landscape architect responsible for Saint Laurent's and Bergé's estate at Deauville, was called in. At Château Gabriel Baecheler had directed the five-year restoration programme that saved it from the derelict state into which it had fallen after the Second World War. The late nineteenth-century château, with murals inspired by Monet's *Water Lilies* and a winter garden containing a forest of ferns and orchids, now looks out over one of the most celebrated private gardens in Normandy. Among the rolling hills a Japanese garden, a huge *potager*, apple orchards and a woodland stream bordered with Louisiana irises, *I. fulva*, create a series of images of different periods and places.

Faced with the heavy clay soil of the Paris site, Baecheler opted for hardy evergreens, which have grown up to form the curtain of green that Saint Laurent had requested. Enclosing the terrace he planted thickets of holly, Irish yews, *Taxus baccata* 'Fastigiata', and spotted laurel, interplanted with large-leaved ivies, viburnums and small flowering camellias, to create a dense undergrowth of contrasting shapes and heights in virtually every shade of green.

The planted areas are bordered, and visually contained, by low wooden trellises, which recall the latticework fences so typical of medieval walled gardens, and which were depicted in the illustrated manuscripts of the period. Here the dark green trellises heighten the sense of formality of the arena-like space

Above, the garden's far perimeter path is lined with formal urns.

Opposite, a seventeenth-century Minotaur is placed between the classically-shaped stone benches.

worked with Saint Laurent on a number of other projects. Bodin provided a strong design which slots neatly into the space available. Centrally placed against the garden façade, a stepped, travertine, semi-circular terrace projects into the garden like the stage of a Roman amphitheatre. The polished surface immediately became a

A late nineteenth-century,
black-and-white bust of a
Bedouin is set into the
rough stone wall and
surrounded by ferns and
ivy.

A striking abstract
sculpture standing in a
mass of foliage is an eye-
catching focal point, placed
at the end of one of the
garden's evergreen-lined
paths.

Delicate strawberries grow
along the low trellis that
lines one of the garden's
many paths.

and surrounding beds, while playing on the
architectural treatment of the space. In
another gesture towards architectural
shapes, four standard *Thuja occidentalis*
mark the step up to the raised platform and
flank the Minotaur. Their near-perfect
spheres, borne on tall, slender trunks, add a
classically French note while at the same
time giving added height to the front edge of
the garden.

Colour is provided on a seasonal basis,
according to a schedule drawn up by Baecheler, by pots of flowering shrubs brought in
regularly from the greenhouses and gardens
at Château Gabriel. In spring a vivid ribbon
of scarlet azaleas threads its way between
the curved balustrade and the trellis, to be
replaced once their flowering period is over
by deep crimson hydrangeas. As summer
turns to autumn the large flower heads dry
on the bushes, making a delicate pattern of
russet and dusty brown above the travertine
bench and against evergreen shrubs behind.
And in winter the view from the apartment's
windows is brightened by tubs of pure white
camellias, which create sudden contrasts
against the dark background.

A neutral-coloured gravel path leads from
either end of the terrace to skirt the perimeter of the square plot. As the visitor
wanders through the seemingly impenetrable evergreen forest, the white-painted
façade is completely swallowed up, and an
atmosphere of romantic abandon takes over.

Hidden in a corner a nineteenth-century
black-and-white marble bust of a Bedouin
rests among the jade-green fronds of ferns
and ivy, like a nomad in an oasis.

Statues are always a feature of Saint
Laurent's gardens, whether to close vistas or
as an element of surprise, to enliven shady
green borders. Among the urns, fountain
heads and other statues at Château Gabriel is
a life-size terracotta female figure, personify-
ing summer. The startled visitor will be
surprised to come across her repeatedly, in
no fewer than seven different positions

throughout the park, as if she too were enjoying an afternoon walk. Lack of space prevented Saint Laurent from using the same technique in his Paris garden, where instead he has placed along the paths a number of half-columns supporting terra-cotta pots. Planted with box and yew, these engender a sense of continuity without being either obvious or too strictly formal; instead they evoke the dreamlike atmosphere of Cocteau's *La Belle et la Bête*.

Roosting in the dappled shade at opposite ends of the gleaming white terrace, pairs of dove-white marble chairs in the form of birds, designed by François-Xavier Lalanne, increase the sense of surrealist mystery that cloaks this lush green garden, which with its combination of the formal with the informal, is a rare blend of mannerism and romanticism.

The formal design of the terrace contrasts with the far reaches of the garden, which is deliberately filled with a profusion of growth.

7

A GARDEN
FULL OF ROMANTICISM

M. and Mme Pierre Landolt
XVIIIe arrondissement

Little would the army of tourists who annually toil up the steep streets of Montmartre to the Sacré Coeur suspect that just a few metres away from the Place du Tertre lies one of the richest and most adventurous gardens in Paris. Clinging to the slopes just below the crest of the Butte, high above the rest of the city, M. and Mme Pierre Landolt's garden is a series of terraces linked by narrow paths and steps and filled with an extraordinary array of plants and picturesque features. Both it and the rambling two-storey house, which dates from 1845, have long

associations with the artistic community which has colonized this airy, light-filled *quartier* since the nineteenth century. The delightfully rural character of the house is enhanced by a graceful spiral staircase with an elegantly curving roof.

In 1905 the painter and engraver Marcel Neumont made a number of alterations and additions in the flamboyant style then fashionable. He added a vast, top-storey south-facing studio overlooking the city, and decorated every surface, inside and out, with representations of his favourite creature, the owl. He displayed equal verve in tackling the garden, which he transformed into a miniature park, with sloping, irregularly shaped beds descending a series of terraces, with meandering paths and flights of steps leading from one level to the next. A stream cascaded through a series of long narrow pools, fed from a waterfall in a grotto; in a secluded corner, hidden from view, was an elaborate aviary; and a tunnel-like flight of shady, overgrown steps linked the bottom terrace to the garden gate, which, obscured by a virtually impenetrable curtain of ivy, opened onto the street below. Bordered by the house at the top and the street far below, and flanked on one side by a wide flight of steps leading to the Place du Tertre and on the other by a strip of woodland, the garden was – and still is – an entirely self-contained little world.

Left, large white and purple blooms of a rhododendron surround a late seventeenth-century bust.

Previous page left, the stone female figure adds a note of serenity amidst the colourful growth.

Previous page right, one of a pair of sphinx in front of which flourishes a mass of daffodils.

Shortly after Marcel Neumont's death in 1930, another artist, Louis Icart, moved in. Apart from removing Neumont's beloved owls he left the garden virtually unchanged, adding only eighteenth-century stone sphinxes, a few classical, carved urns and busts of himself and Madame Icart, watching over each other from opposite sides of one of the paths.

By the time M. and Mme Landolt arrived (incidentally continuing the artistic tradition, as Pierre Landolt is the grandson of the sculptor Edouard Marcel Sandoz), the garden had quietly disappeared underneath a blanket of vegetation, and the views had become completely obscured by overgrown laurels. Over the past decade, with the help of their friend Jacques Valdi, they have worked to restore the garden to its *fin-de-siècle* exuberance, and to recapture its former magic.

By early May each year the garden façade of the house has vanished behind a tapestry of glossy Boston ivy and the delicate green tendrils of a 'Muscat de Hambourg' grapevine, while the spiral staircase is festooned with *Wisteria sinensis*. A Japanese pagoda

tree, *Sophora japonica*, listed and protected by the authorities, casts a dappled shade over the gravel terrace below, and bears long racemes of delicate creamy-white flowers in August and September.

The large, purple-centred, white heads of *R. sutchuenense* add colour to the gravel courtyard.

In early spring the blossom and the white-flowering cherry seems to float against the dark ivy, and by late spring even the flame-red Mollis azaleas on the terrace are over-shadowed by an enormous *Rhododendron sutchuenense*, laden with purple-centred white flowers.

M. Valdi's planting scheme includes numerous different varieties with flowering periods lasting for anything from several weeks to just a few hours, depending on weather conditions in this exposed site. In spring, for example, strong sunlight or harsh, drying winds to which the garden is prone can burn the hundreds of narcissi planted in drifts of different varieties: 'Geranium', 'Fortune' and 'Tudor Minstrel', to name only a few. Yet M. Valdi and the Landolts have incorporated this element of the ephemeral into their concept of the garden, exploiting it to create a series of brilliant images, each succeeding the last.

Louis Icart's sphinxes flank the rolling patch of lawn, which is punctuated with a small circular pool and fountain. To the right of the spiral staircase, against the façade of the original part of the house and in the shade of the Japanese pagoda tree, is another water feature: Marcel Neumont's waterfall, like a tiny replica of the grottoes that were so popular in parks such as Vincennes or the Buttes-Chaumont at the end of the nineteenth century. A large water tank collects rainwater from the roof to supply the waterfall, which cascades down the concrete rocks to feed the stream that snakes down the garden. As well as being picturesque this system has its practical advantage, for it is a labour-saving device for supplying water to most parts of the garden.

M. Valdi had the idea of adding a concealed bed around the top rim of the waterfall, which he filled with sweetbriars, *Rosa rubiginosa* 'Patricia'. The cascade of sweet-scented foliage and single red blooms touched with white at the centre, the trickling water and the 'ruined' grotto together

Above, shaded by an ancient *Sophora japonica*, the house's many levels are joined by an open staircase that looks out over the abundant garden growth.

Left, a wide sweep of lilies of the valley banks the narrow pools that cut across the garden. Beyond, busts of the former owners, the French artist Louis Icart and his wife regard each other across a steep stone staircase.

form an intensely romantic combination. In the darker recesses of the waterfall moisture-loving ferns and ivies flourish in the crevices in the rock. The rare, wavy-leaved ivy, *Hedera helix* 'Triton', weaves among Hart's

Left, in spring the paths that lead through the sloping site are bordered with vivid splashes of colour which contrast with the evergreens in the central area. A pink-flowering syringa contrasts with the golden-green elaeagnus, while a tall stone column smothered in ivy increases the sense of height.

Right, concealed in the garden's lower reaches and screened from the street below by a wall of Virginia creeper, a bed is planted with a collection of over a hundred different varieties of iris.

tongue ferns, *Phyllitis scolopendrium*, while the small-leaved, almost black *H. h.* 'Pedata' ivy creeps round clumps of *Woodsia ilvensis* ferns. In late summer, when the terrace is exposed to full sun throughout the day, one of the most pleasant spots in the garden is beside the waterfall, where a refreshing cool mist hangs in the warm air.

In spring an oval bed set into the lawn is filled with blue and white hyacinths, oxalis, drifts of narcissi and daffodils, and yellow tulips. By early summer the bed is a mass of yellow, white and red as a collection of Hybrid tea roses come into bloom, including *R.* 'Fimbriata' and *R.* 'Proflera de Redouté'. Below, the grassy bank flows down to a drift of lilies-of-the-valley interplanted with blue-bells. Growing larger every year, this patch of mauve and white flowers and fresh pale green leaves is a charming contrast to the bed of dark ivy which it has replaced.

On the other side of the pools grow bushes of *Callicarpa japonica*, Japanese beauty-berry, their striking metallic-purple berries reflected in the water in late autumn, after the leaves have fallen. Massed orange and deep-yellow tulips, 'Dillenburg' and 'Mary Housley', are succeeded by spreading hostas and dicentras. A tall, red, horse chestnut, *Aesculus* x *carnea*, used to cast a dense shade over the area until M. Valdi recommended that it be pruned and stripped of the ivy that had climbed into it and threatened to strangle it. With its attractive panicles of rose-pink flowers, enhancing the view both from the garden and from the house, it would have been too great a loss, so drastic action was taken.

Sitting on an ivy-covered plinth, a black marble statue of a girl by M. Landolt's grandfather seems to be backlit by a large *Elaeagnus pungens* 'Aurea'. Scenting the air in early spring is a newly planted *Viburnum carlesii*, its highly fragrant clusters of small star-shaped white flowers appearing to float against the shady background. Further down the bank a pink-tinged lilac flowers near white and purple varieties of buddleia, which attract hundreds of butterflies later in summer. Their loose arching habit contrasts with the columnar fastigiate Japanese cherry, *Prunus serrulata* 'Amanogawa', which in spring is covered with a mass of semi-double light pink blossom. Bright pink cactus dahlias fill the corner in summer, silhouetted against a deep green yew, one of the few remaining in the garden, while clumps of pale yellow Welsh poppies take the place of the drifts of bluebells and white muscari along the path. In autumn the beds are filled with luminous yellow *Sternbergia lutea*, flowering among the sword-like leaves of *Anemone sylvestris*, which bears its deli-

cate white flowers the following spring. Clumps of tall aquilegias, deep blue monkshood, *Aconitum napellus*, and rich yellow day lilies add further colour in late summer; and throughout the summer this luxuriant display is set off by the arching, fine-toothed fronds of royal ferns, *Osmunda regalis*, up to two metres high.

The busts of M. Icart and his wife eye each other closely across the narrow path, Monsieur rising sternly from the glossy leaves of the mound of *Acanthus mollis*, while tendrils of variegated ivy, *Hedera helix* 'Goldheart', twine around Madame's plinth. Purple-flowering *Campanula portenschlagiana* cascades down and across the brick steps below them, while under the red-tinged leaves of a group of mahonias small mounds of candytuft, *Iberis saxatilis*, glow white from May to July.

On the bottom terrace overlooking the street, the large aviary cage set into the hillside by Marcel Neumont has been completely restored. It is now home to a pair of Chinese mandarin ducks, the drake's rich blue and brown plumage easily outshining the female's and adding a touch of exotic colour to the garden. For M. Landolt the birds recall his grandfather's studio in Montparnasse, where the intrepid M. Sandoz kept a large menagerie of wild animals to serve as models, including a lion, a bear, and a flock of mandarin ducks. Beside the aviary is the children's play area, with a square lawn and a sandpit. Rosemary and sweet bay, *Laurus nobilis*, stand at the entrance to the space, while the far edge is bordered by a double row of irises which are only a tiny selection from one of the garden's chief glories: the collection of over a hundred different varieties of iris laid out in long rows in the neighbouring bed. M. Valdi has added a number of unusual varieties and colourings, including the pale grey and black mourning iris, *Iris susiana*. Subtle groupings of colours include the chocolate-brown 'Velvet Robe', bronze-peach 'Olympic Torch', deep brown

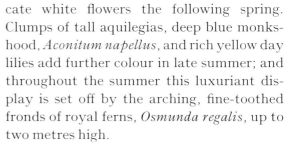

Sculpted by Edouard Marcel Sandoz, M. Landolt's grandfather, the black marble statue glistens after rainfall, surrounded by profuse growths of *Elaeagnus pungens* 'Aurea'.

The abundant growth seems to tumble down the steep garden to the street below.

By early summer the flight of stone steps are engulfed with *Campanula portenschlagiana*.

'Mary Todd' and two-toned 'Gay Parasol'. Tall pink and white hollyhocks rise behind them, while an apple tree, smothered with deep pink blossom in late spring, arches overhead, a ball of mistletoe clinging to its boughs. In such a rural setting it is hard to believe that just the other side of the Boston ivy-covered wall lies a bustling, noisy city street.

In a shady corner, beneath a 'Charles x' lilac spreads a restful carpet of variegated *Vinca major* 'Elegantissima', dotted with delicate flowers in spring and early summer, and bergenia bearing soft pink and purple panicles in spring. Nearby stand some small pots containing new acquisitions: *Poncirus trifoliata* – the hardy orange shrub – a medlar seedling, miniature mahonias, and a collection of small-leaved, variegated ivies. Soon, like their predecessors, a *Viburnum davidii* and *Deutzia gracilis* – both with white flowers in May and June – and the winter-flowering jasmine *J. nudiflorum*, they will find their place in the garden.

Few gardens contain such a variety of plants and *jeux d'esprit* combined with such careful regard for the aesthetics of the overall scheme. The inspiration of Marcel Neumont and the dedication of M. and Mme Landolt and Jacques Valdi have together produced a unique ever-changing garden, full of surprises and delights for plantsmen and romantics alike.

8

A TINY GARDEN
OF BAMBOO

VIIe arrondissement

This tiny city garden, hidden behind the imposing sculpted stone façades of the Rue de Varenne, in the *VIIe arrondissement*, is tucked away half way down a tree-lined private cul-de-sac. Wedged in a small pocket between the splendid eighteenth-century *hôtels* of the Faubourg Saint-Germain, is a small thicket of cool, airy greenery, framed against a background of tall, luxuriant bamboo. After a series of attempts to make a more traditional garden in the limited space, all more or less unsuccessful, the owners, with the help of the garden designer Robert

Bazelaire, hit on the solution which has transformed this difficult site.

The garden borders the shady lane, hidden from view by a solid two-metre-high dark green fence which cocoons the tiny square plot. The apartment's living room, which also enjoys direct views over the park-like grounds of the embassy next door, gives on to a raised, L-shaped white stone terrace, which borders the garden on two sides and is used in summer for outdoor entertaining. Below it lies the sunken six-metre-square garden, partially shaded by the whitewashed

From the raised terrace and outdoor dining area, the lofty thicket of bamboo creates a light, airy atmosphere with its delicate green shades and the rustling of the canes and leaves.

Wispy low bamboo foliage engulfs the stairway leading from the cool, sparse terrace to the equally refreshing greenery-filled garden below.

Previous page left, scattered throughout the cool bamboo copse, fallen leaves, pebbles and rocks create a subtly shaded ground cover.

Previous page right, although the garden is very small it nevertheless contains an extraordinary variety of bamboo species.

walls of a neighbouring building which looms overhead.

Before consulting M. Bazelaire, the owners tried out their own ideas. First they laid out a *jardin de curé*, a traditional feature throughout rural France and a direct descendant of sixteenth-century planting schemes, where, spilling out of their geometrically ordered beds, flowers, vegetables, herbs and espaliered fruit trees were cultivated side by side in tumbling profusion. This rural scheme seemed to derive added charm from its urban context, but sadly it was not destined to survive in the damp,

shady conditions of the city. Their next idea was inspired by Japanese Zen gardens, such as the Ryoan-ji temple in Kyoto. Accordingly they laid out a ground cover of pebbles, but, unlike the Japanese garden, punctuated the stone arrangements with shrubs clipped into low, round ball-shapes and dwarf conifers. This time the plants survived, but the overall concept of the scheme seemed somehow to have got lost in the execution. At this point they approached M. Bazelaire, who came up with the key to their problems: bamboo, in profusion. It seemed to capture the essence of what the owners really wanted from the garden: masses of greenery without blocking out the precious light.

Bamboo has become the hallmark of Robert Bazelaire's work, whether in Paris or the country. Surprisingly, this beautiful and useful evergreen, which has been cultivated in China and Japan for over two thousand years, has been in general cultivation in the West only since the end of the nineteenth century. Introduced two centuries earlier, for a long time it remained a rarity, used only for its exotic associations in stylized garden features inspired by the craze for chinoiserie. By the end of the nineteenth century a number of specialist bamboo gardens had been established in Europe, with collections of the many varieties discovered and brought back as a result of botanical expeditions to Asia Minor and the Far East. With more than a dozen genera and over seven hundred varieties to be found throughout the world, this giant species of grass has gradually become appreciated more and more for its thick screening properties, its lacy foliage, its architectural form – and of course, for its air of oriental mystery.

In this garden, M. Bazelaire observed to the letter his maxim, 'plant big in small spaces'. After removing the dwarf conifers which disappeared below the ledge of the terrace, he planted substantial stands of *Phyllostachys viridi-glaucescens*, which grows to a height of nine metres. With it he planted clumps of two other varieties: rare black bamboo, *Phyllostachys nigra*, from southern China, and low-growing Japanese kumazasa, *Sasa veitchii*. When planted in partial shade, as here, the kumazasa grows to only two metres, about half its normal height in a sunny position. Here its pale green foliage arches gracefully over the stone steps leading down into the well of the garden, softening the hard surfaces. Viewed from the terrace or inside the apartment it seems to billow and foam like a leafy wave underneath the black bamboo.

The foliage of the two taller varieties creates a filmy, multi-layered effect through which the light filters softly. For M. Bazelaire the bamboos fulfil many functions: 'Since the terrace was raised above the deep wall of the garden it was important to have something tall. Another reason I use bamboo is for its light, airy effects. And for me the slight murmuring of the leaves as they sway in the wind, and the delicate shadows they cast seem to have a symbolic, almost mystical significance.'

Another Japanese native which thrives in the dappled shade is *Acer palmatum*, the spectacular Japanese maple, of which M. Bazelaire planted three varieties. One of the few deciduous trees traditionally permitted in Japanese tea gardens, the small-leaved native maple is customarily included in these small enclosures because of its strong associations with the natural vegetation of the hillsides surrounding Kyoto, where the tea ceremony is supposed to have originated. The ritual of the tea ceremony brought together men of different social classes, warriors and nobles, in a ritual designed to purify the mind and spirit. Guests indulged in high-minded conversation, from which all mention of business and politics was prohibited, and drank a variety of special and unusual teas, which they were asked to identify. By the fifteenth century the ritual had been refined and elaborated to the point where every aspect of the environment in

Above, a traditional Japanese *tsukubai* or water basin stands at the base of the stairway leading to the garden.

Left, a split-bamboo fence conceals the concrete wall of the terrace and leads the eye from the garden to the raised level above.

which it was held and the utensils to be used were prescribed in minute detail, which also had a direct effect on Japanese garden design. Planted here are the translucent bronze-red *Acer palmatum* 'Atropurpurem', *A. p.* 'Scolopendrifolium', characterized by its narrow green deeply lobed leaves, and the graceful threadleaf maple *A. p.* 'Dissectum

Right, the variety of
ground cover together with
the irregular, natural
bamboo plantings give the
garden the impression of
being larger than it is, with
unexpected discoveries at
every step.

Ornatum', with delicate lacy foliage which casts a gauzy shade. Hidden from sight until the visitor is right on top of the garden, these three delicate shrubs add decorative touches of brilliant scarlet to the evergreen composition. The limited number of plant types employed in the small space create an endless series of patterns as their dead foliage blankets the river-washed stones.

At the bottom of the steps stands another of the tea masters' contributions to Japanese garden design, a *tsukubai*, or water basin, this one assembled by Bazelaire himself. An important feature of the tea ceremony, the *tsukubai* has its origins in the custom of placing a pitcher of water on a rock near the entry to the garden. As they arrived guests would wash their hands to symbolize the cleansing of their thoughts before they encountered the other participants in the ceremony. In time it became a permanent feature, usually set in a 'sea' or bed of small pebbles or sand, with water supplied via hollow bamboo poles. To complete the tranquil picture M. Bazelaire has added a wooden ladle resting on top of the stone basin.

The concrete foundations of the terrace's retaining wall are covered by a split bamboo fence in the Kennin-ji-gaki style, one of the many traditional Japanese designs for fences, which emphasizes the garden's vertical lines and harmonizes with the plants. Japanese gardeners devised many variations on the theme of fencing, mostly using twine and bamboo, which were valued for the important role they played in creating an appropriate atmosphere for the tea gardens. Other materials included brushwood, cedar, and cypress, and, for the semi-transparent partitions between different spaces, lighter materials such as bamboo shavings and wisteria vines. The relationship between these materials and the plants assumed greater significance in the design of the private areas of the gardens, intended to lead the visitor's imagination out of the material world and on to a higher plane.

While many of the theories that governed traditional Japanese garden design are apparent here, M. Bazelaire never intended or even hoped to re-create a tea garden like those in Japan: 'It would be impossible for me or anyone who was not Japanese to create a truly Japanese environment. All I can do is work in accordance with their basic ideas and principles of garden design, for I share a great love of their native plants. Above all I respect their fascination with the opposing forces of wildness and domestication.'

At first glance the bamboos and maples here seem to be growing in conditions that approach as nearly as possible, given the confines of the site, their natural state. But on closer inspection it becomes apparent that, as in all M. Bazelaire's gardens, every aspect is carefully controlled and organized to produce the maximum number of different effects. Meticulous planning and calculations and conscientious pruning and training lie behind this extraordinarily evocative landscape. Even the dead leaves create their effect, washing like a rustling brown waterfall around and over the river-washed pebbles.

Limited as much by its modest dimensions as by its austerely restricted range of materials, this small, quiet space provides a rare and refreshing experience, both sensual and spiritual, for those who are receptive to it. While many gardens, and particularly classical French gardens, seem to be based on the premise of man's domination over nature, which they demonstrate at every turn, this one expresses an attitude which is fundamentally different.

With the changing of the seasons, and even of conditions from day to day or hour to hour, this garden assumes nature's not man's correspondingly varied moods. Gentle breezes and strong winds, overcast light and bright sunshine, all are expressed in the swaying stands of the softly murmuring bamboo.

9

A MINIMALIST WALLED GARDEN

M. and Mme Eric Germain
XVe arrondissement

Eric and Xiane Germain's walled garden, spare and simple to the point of minimalism, provokes from visitors reactions ranging from delighted astonishment to puzzled confusion: 'When are you going to start planting?' they ask. Designed by French *paysagiste* Alain Richert from the remnants of the existing twenty-year-old layout, this space resists definition as a 'garden' in the traditional sense, and is rather an abstraction of – and play on – the fundamental elements of any garden: light, earth and water. In defiance of current fashions in garden design it

explores the qualities of each component at the expense of abundant planting. Stripped down to their basics, these create a pared-down, non-naturalistic composition, always stimulating to look at, and a fitting extension to the contemporary design of the Germains' house.

The three-storey building stands on the Rue Dombasle in the *XVe arrondissement*, south-west of the city centre. The street appears on maps published as early as 1737, and was once part of the *commune* or village of Vaugirard. By the mid-nineteenth cen-

tury, like many of the *communes* that encircled Paris, Vaugirard found itself sandwiched between two rings of fortifications. Only a few gatehouses or *portes* now survive from the earlier walls, designed by Charles Nicolas Ledoux for Louis XVI in 1784–7. The outer defences, known as the 'Thiers' wall after the veteran conservative politician Adolphe Thiers, were thrown up in 1841–4, in the turmoil between the revolutions of 1789 and 1848. In 1859 the *chambre des députés* voted to absorb the land between the two barricades into the metropolitan area, and Vaugirard and three other *communes* became part of Paris. These newly incorporated areas lagged far behind the rest of Paris in the provision of urban amenities such as paved roads and street lighting. While these arrived in due course, the *XVe arrondissement* has never quite lost its slower pace of life.

A mysterious, dark, narrow passageway off the Rue Dombasle marks the entrance to the Germains' house. It leads from the cobbled street to a raised terrace, half-hidden by foliage, from which the garden first becomes visible. At each end of the terrace a pair of concrete steps leads down into the sunken area below. This is flanked by forbiddingly high rendered brick walls, framing the glass-fronted house at the far end.

The house was designed in 1970 by the noted interior designer Pierre Garriche, a professor at the Académie des Beaux-Arts whose work, including a great many interiors and a variety of furniture, came to typify 1960s design. The two-storey structure mirrors the site's strongly linear composition, with the long vertical lines of its two terraces now wreathed with fresh green Virginia creeper. Garriche's sleek use of brilliantly reflective materials, from the white marble terrace to the sliding glass panels that make up the façade of the house, has a crisply contemporary feel, though the design is now twenty years old. Its uncompromising modernism, set in a modest suburban context,

appealed immediately to the Germains.

They were less captivated, however, by the garden, which they found sad and lifeless, as Xiane Germain recalls: 'It seemed like a walled pit one had to cross in order to reach the light-filled house at the other end. There were a few tufts of grass struggling for life, a depressing birch and overgrown forsythia everywhere. The garden seemed neither to soften the rigid nature of the space nor to complement its linear composition. Inside the house there is a constant play of light, but this was completely lost in the dark and drab exterior space.' They decided that the garden needed to be restructured in such a way as to capture the spirit of the house, and invited the landscape designer, Alain Richert, an old friend, to come and look at the site.

The remarkable variety of Richert's work is an indication of the strength of his com-

Above, at the base of one wall M. Richert planted evergreen shrubs.

Opposite, the terrace, apartment and garden are studies in the use of simple horizontal and vertical lines.

Previous page left, by training honeysuckle to grow up poles Catherine Willis created an effective covering for the wall at the garden's far end.

Previous page right, the terrace, the paved area below and the steps that join the two emphasize the garden's sparse design.

mitment to, and passion for, his craft, whatever the scale and context of a commission – whether for an august body such as the Caisse Nationale des Monuments Historiques et des Sites or for private clients such as the Germains. His skill as a plantsman, combined with a comprehensive knowledge of the historical background and his own unusual flair, allows him to break away from the more conventional models of garden design, and to create gardens which are truly contemporary and not merely a hotchpotch of old styles adapted to new uses. He is particularly intrigued by the relationship between house and garden and by the nature of the space that articulates between the two, which is sometimes a garden and sometimes not. Accordingly he feels his next step is to design both together.

Richert's first commission was for one of France's most influential gardens: Villandry on the Loire, aptly described by Hugh Johnson as 'the ultimate kitchen garden'. His task was to replace the bedding plants that filled the elaborate pattern of geometrically arranged beds with plants contemporary with the sixteenth-century château. The result rather shocked the public, who were used to the traditional, brightly coloured schemes. Other projects with a strong historical context, but into which he yet manages to inject an element of fun and magic, include a commission to create a medieval garden around an impregnable fortress keep, also in the Loire valley. He has also undertaken work at the sixteenth- and seventeenth-century Château d'Eu near Dieppe, where in gardens originally designed by Le Nôtre, he created, among other things, an island orchard; and one of his most recent large-scale commissions was on the shores of Lake Geneva. Here he planted a maze of hornbeam and espaliered fruit trees, a magical combination which encloses a series of square plots with planting dedicated to the five senses. Unlike the work of other garden designers, Richert's projects, both public

The sharp, clean lines of the garden's composition are broken only by the light that sparkles from the water troughs and by the tiny bamboo leaves scattered on the bare earth.

and private, tend to remain open to the general view, a principle he strongly defends.

When he was called in by the Germains three years ago, Richert's initial response to the garden, which had remained unchanged since 1970, was to strip it down to the bare framework and begin again. He explains his rationale thus: 'So often garden design is governed by an overwhelming sense of puritanical prudishness. Bare, raw earth is seen as untidy and rather embarrassing, and people feel compelled to cover its nakedness with spreading ground cover. So many gardens today are zealously over-planted, apparently in an attempt to create an approximation of a sort of prehistoric jungle, with the result that the individuality of each plant is swamped and its beauty lost. Here, although it was a difficult space, I wanted to capture some of the feeling of luminosity and weightlessness attached to the house.'

Once the site had been cleared, with only the stone path, embedded as it was in solid concrete foundations, left in place, Richert introduced a selection of flowering evergreen shrubs. Lining the space on either side he planted a row of tall maples and plane trees at regular intervals. Their straight dark trunks, silhouetted against the Virginia

The striking simplicity of the garden's design is seen to best advantage when viewed from the house's terrace. The water in the four narrow troughs captures the light, sparkling against the backdrop of overhanging branches.

creeper which cloaks the walls on both sides, emphasize the linear composition of the space. At the far end, beside the white marble terrace, an acacia casts a soft shade.

Along one wall, between the entrance steps and the house, Richert planted repeating groups of shrubs which flower at different times of year. The unusual *Osmarea burkwoodii*, a cross between *Phillyrea decora* and the fragrant *Osmanthus delavayi*, produces clusters of sweetly-scented white flowers in late April, and its deep green foliage provides a dramatic contrast with small mounds of *Viburnum davidii*, chosen for their pearl-like berries, which appear (if male and female plants are grown together) after the white flowers in late autumn. Clumps of Mexican orange, *Choisya ternata*, also provide interest throughout the year, for their glossy evergreen foliage is highly aromatic when crushed, and in May and recurrently throughout the summer and autumn they bear their white star-shaped flowers, which give off an intoxicating scent.

Along the edge of the terrace Richert planted another fragrant evergreen bush which will eventually be clipped to make a rectangular-shaped hedge to echo the shape

Splashes of colour in this minimalist garden are provided by two bright yellow garden chairs laid out on the terrace.

of the terrace's wide, low edge: holly osmanthus, *O. heterophyllus*, the only scented flowering evergreen that takes to pruning and will still produce a strong perfume, the flowers being borne on the previous year's growth. On the other side of the terrace, near to the kitchen door is the American hybrid holly, *Ilex* 'Blue James', also destined to be a hedge. Richert employed this recent intro-duction for its rapid growth and distinctive purple-tinged branches that can withstand heavy pruning.

Along the edge of the terrace, dotted around the garden, and against the wall beside the house Richert planted clumps of Chinese black bamboo, *Phyllostachys nigra*, which breaks the garden's perpendicular lines with their gracefully arching stems.

Their airy tufts of foliage soften the severity of the design, and in autumn and winter some of the leaves turn yellow and fall, catching the light and creating golden patterns against the rich dark earth.

From the straight black trunks of a row of four hornbeams, *Carpinus betulus*, Catherine Willis, an artist, writer, accomplished gardener and friend of both Richert and the Germains, suspended a trellis made from two long carbon-fibre rods, along which she has trained fronds of honeysuckle. The tendrils of pale green foliage and sweet-scented flowers strike a pleasantly unruly note against the garden's strong horizontal and vertical lines.

In the central part of the garden Richert laid out the water feature which seems to cast a spell over the entire area. Into the bare earth he sank four narrow, black-painted, rectangular troughs, with the water level flush with the ground, and far enough away from the house to be visible from inside. Day and night, the water surface is alive with light and movement, shimmering in the slightest breeze and rippling as the birds come to drink or bathe. Where a traditional *miroir d'eau* in a classical French garden would reflect large expanses of blue sky and scudding clouds, these small pools create a flickering, kaleidoscopic display of fragmented, splintering images that seem to ricochet like reflected sunbeams around the sunken space. At night, when the garden is lit by the beams of three airport runway lamps, dramatically positioned flush with the ground, the light seems to reverberate between the illuminated branches of overhanging trees and the thin strips of silvery water, and the garden, reflected in the glass façade of the house, appears to double in size.

The garden's most constant yet ever-changing feature is the bare earth. When soaked with rain it becomes rich and heavy, while after a brief dry spell it is transformed into translucent layers of fine powdery dust. Never the same from one season to the next,

the soil creates a warm, textured background for the garden's linear forms. In most gardens such architectural features are set in or against dense planting, designed to anchor the structure, and visually to smooth the transition between the two. Here, Richert deliberately did the opposite, setting out to create a momentarily unsettling, uneasy effect, designed to encourage the viewer unconsciously to focus a little more clearly.

While this remarkable garden, so conceptual in approach, may challenge human assumptions about garden design, it immediately became home to hundreds of local birds. They make themselves entirely at home, swooping and chattering and adding a delightfully unexpected and random note to Alain Richert's carefully and sensitively considered design.

The tall verticals of black bamboo, *Phyllostachys nigra*, heighten the minimalist plan with their dark, straight shoots, while their light, airy leaves break the formal composition, preventing it from appearing too sombre.

10

A Garden of Favourite Flowers

Mme Marcelle Galia
VIIIᵉ arrondissement

Marcelle Galia's charmingly small-scale garden was conceived as a deliberately modest antechamber to the remains of one of the most extravagant horticultural confections that Paris has ever seen, the Parc Monceau. Shortly after she moved into her ground-floor apartment in the *VIIIᵉ arrondissement*, on one of the few streets that border the park, Mme Galia learned that she was even more fortunate than she had realized. For a gardening neighbour informed her that while the other gardens in the street had the benefit of the park's magnificent mature

trees as a backdrop, hers alone had direct views on to it. Where her neighbours backed on to dense shrubberies or tall fences, she was able to enjoy the light, airy prospect of its serpentine paths and picturesque vistas, its architectural conceits and its shady groves of broad-leaved trees.

The garden itself, however, was a sad anticlimax: 'When I first arrived here, the garden didn't look anything like it does today. There was an awful-looking patch of weedy grass and an equally miserable-looking laurel hedge surrounding the whole

Left, detail of a stone cross dated 1255 that stands at one end of the stone terrace.

Previous page left, beyond the rectangular sweep of lawn towering trees from the Parc Monceau shade this intimate Parisian garden. Contrasting with the trees' dark green foliage, fresh, light green bamboo shoots mark the garden's northern edge.

Previous page right, the rare oak-leaved *Hydrangea quercifolia* – a favourite of Mme Galia's – was planted against the low wall of the garden terrace and is highlighted with vivid tufts of impatiens and delicate-flowering rose bushes.

garden. The only good thing about those dreadful laurels was their scarlet berries, which were the garden's only touch of colour in winter. But that wasn't enough to convince me and I quickly tore them out. Along with the open views of the park I could also peer down and enjoy my neighbour's garden on the left – just as they could mine, which I didn't find terribly agreeable. What I loved most was the garden's rolling movement down towards those unexpected vistas.' As she began to rethink the garden, the park yielded another unexpected advantage in the form of its team of gardeners and their considerable expertise and experience, which they were happy to share with her: 'If I wasn't quite sure just how a plant might do here, or where to find a certain variety, I just headed down to the garden gate, leant over and asked.'

The park was originally laid out in 1778 as the private pleasure gardens of the Duc d'Orléans. By the second half of the century the theories governing French garden design had gone through an evolutionary process that resulted in a new set of standards and ideals vastly different from those of previous generations. Gone were the principles by which Le Nôtre had laid out the Sun King's grandiose gardens in the late seventeenth century, where order and balance, monumental perspectives and geometrical symmetry were employed to rationalize spaces that progressed in logical sequence towards meticulously calculated vanishing points. Gone, too, was the man whose absolute power was reaffirmed with every step within the royal confines. Visitors to Versailles were no longer instructed to follow the garden guide written, and twice revised, by Louis XIV himself, which set out an itinerary complete with minute instructions on how the gardens were to be viewed, from which exact points the perspectives were to be marvelled at, and the angles from which the allegorical statues were to be admired. Watteau, Boucher and Fragonard were the harbingers of change in the world of painting and the landscapes in their works testify to the new taste for romantic abandonment and picturesque dereliction. In literature Rousseau, in *La Nouvelle Héloise*, published in 1761, encouraged the idea of the garden as a place where nature should be allowed to have its way, untrammelled and unfettered. It was the English landscape movement, meanwhile, which showed how such bucolic fantasies could be realized on the ground. 'Natural' landscapes of serpentine lakes and streams meandering past gentle hillocks, smooth green swards and oppositely placed copses appeared as if miraculously on aristocratic estates all over England and quickly spread to the Continent. Meanwhile the English craze for all things pastoral became joined in a rather eclectic marriage with a new taste for exoticism, and particularly chinoiserie. The result was termed by the French 'le style anglo-chinois'. Examples of the imaginative notions of Chinese garden design then prevalent were published between 1767 and 1783 by Georges-Louis Le Rouge in his *Détails des nouveaux jardins à la mode: jardins anglo-chinois*. The engravings of plans, elevations and perspective views showed examples of English, French and German gardens, such as the 'project for an English garden by the Prince de Croÿ on his return from London', with pages of alternative designs for grottoes, bridges, pavilions, temples and the full gamut of picturesque features or *fabriques*. The anthology also included over one thousand plates of the Emperor of China's private gardens, Chinese temple sites and mountain monasteries, all of which held a strong fascination for the gardening public.

Yet ironically these naturalistic landscapes were just as artificially conceived and many times as labour intensive as the gardens that went before. An impressive array of *fabriques*, from Chinese pagodas to Corinthian colonnades, and from Egyptian pyramids to Tartar tents, became *de rigueur*, for a promenade round such a garden intended to evoke reactions from all points in the emotional spectrum, from awe in the face of the sublime to delight at some pretty, frivolous concoction. The Parc Monceau, designed

The red-flowering rose stands against a contrasting backdrop of deep green foliage.

Yellow-flowering rhododendrons and hydrangeas thrive in the bed sheltered by the ivy-covered wall of the neighbouring garden.

The stone terrace that runs the length of the ground-floor apartment affords spectacular views across the garden to the vast Parc Monceau.

Hydrangea paniculata grows up supporting poles to allow other plants to grow underneath, thus filling the small plot to best advantage.

by Carmontelle, was among the first of these *jardins anglo-chinois*, and although it has been greatly reduced in size and altered over the years, it still retains some of the innumerable *fabriques* originally placed there for the delight of Louis-Philippe d'Orléans, Duc de Chartres, a dedicated anglophile and friend of the Prince of Wales, the future Prince Regent and George IV.

A painting by Carmontelle depicts the young nobleman receiving the keys to his newly created garden from its designer. While the two figures congratulate each other, hard-working gardeners are planting up the banks of a winding stream. In the middle distance various groups disport themselves, some pausing in the shade of a gnarled tree by a ruined temple, while others, crossing a stone bridge, watch a man lazily fishing in the lake below. In the hazy distance the outlines of a Gothic pavilion, windmills and an antique column can be discerned. An afternoon's walk in the garden took the visitor on a whirlwind tour of Greece, China, Holland, Italy and Egypt, by way of forests, meadows, lakes and brooks. Among the *fabriques* that have not survived are an Italian vineyard, Dutch windmills, a grotto-greenhouse-dining room and – an unusual feature for the time – a colour garden, composed of a circular central area surrounded by three flower gardens each planted exclusively in yellow, red or blue.

The gardens were confiscated during the Revolution, and despite rechristening himself Philippe-Egalité and voting for the death of his cousin Louis XVI, its illustrious owner did not escape the guillotine during the Reign of Terror. From the Revolution until the Restoration, when it was returned to Philippe-Egalité's son, the future King Louis-Philippe, the garden became a public amusement park, and many of the features were turned into paying attractions.

In 1852 the city of Paris took possession of just under half the park's original nineteen hectares, which nine years later were restructured and as far as possible restored by Jean-Charles-Adolphe Alphand, who also worked on the Bois de Boulogne and the Buttes-Chaumont. The rest of the land was parcelled up and sold off to rich merchants and bankers and the affluent middle classes who constructed grand *hôtel particuliers* and apartment houses in the lavish style of the Second Empire.

At the bottom of Mme Galia's gently sloping site a small metal gate opens directly onto the park, an extremely rare feature in any Parisian garden. At the top of the garden is a terrace paved in white stone and edged with narrow beds, filled in summer with white and salmon-pink impatiens. Three wide travertine steps, placed on axis with the gate leading into the park, lead down into the garden. They are flanked by columnar Irish yews, *Taxus baccata* 'Fastigiata', which frame the views from inside the apartment.

Two wide beds running the width of the terrace either side are planted with different varieties of hydrangea, one of Mme Galia's favourite plants. The flowers and foliage of the common hydrangea, *H. macrophylla*, billow above the terrace, contrasting with the dark, glossy ivy that clothes the railings behind. In midsummer *H. m.* 'Altona' bears its large, rounded rose-pink blooms, while on the other side of the steps, just outside the main salon window, are two different white-flowering varieties. One is the unusual oak-leaved hydrangea, *H. quercifolia*, originally from the south-eastern states of north America and first discovered in the late eighteenth century. The flowers, borne in erect panicles, appear in July, and the large, lobed leaves turn brilliant scarlet in autumn, complementing the rich autumn colour of the park below. Above these, and in direct view of the apartment, are three tall *H. paniculata* 'Grandiflora', with pyramidal panicles up to forty-five centimetres long. Both varieties are normally bushy in habit and so it proved impossible to plant them next to each other in the limited space available until Mme Galia discovered a standard form of the 'Grandiflora'.

Down the northern side of the garden, in contrast with the ivy-clad railings opposite, is a light-textured wall of bamboo, which simultaneously screens the next-door garden and draws the eye to the vista over the park. The tall clumps of Chinese hedge bamboo, *Bambusa multiplex* 'Fernleaf', rustle gently in the slightest breeze, adding a note of airy grace to the garden.

In order not to disturb the exceptional views, Mme Galia decided to keep the garden's central area open, so she reseeded and rolled the lawn, and at the bottom planted groups of late May-flowering rhododendrons. Pruned occasionally so that it does not impinge on the vista, the evergreen shrubbery disguises the difference in levels and softens the transition between the garden and the park. As in most of the rest of the garden, Mme Galia limited the colours here to muted pastel shades; 'Except for the climbing rose on the mushroom-shaped frame, I haven't used any vivid red for the flowers in the garden. For the rhododendrons I finally chose a soft blend of light pastel colours. Even white, let alone red, would have been too harsh against the view behind.' They include 'Elspeth', with rose-pink buds fading to pale pink, bell-shaped pale pink 'Temple Belle' and, providing a contrasting touch of yellow, 'Crest'.

Mme Galia's garden is a lesson in tact and understatement. Wisely, she has not attempted to compete with the splendours of the park beyond, but instead has set out systematically to create an unobtrusive foil for them. She has been so successful that in doing so she has added greatly to the soothing, gentle charms of her own garden, the perfect place from which to observe the drama of the Duc d'Orléan's pleasure grounds.

'The only splash of red I use in the garden comes from the small scarlet blossoms of the climbing rose,' says Mme Galia of the magnificent bush that stands alone in one corner of the lawn.

II

A SHADY YEW GARDEN

Mme Charlotte Aillaud
VIIᵉ arrondissement

Charlotte Aillaud's peaceful *hôtel particulier* and garden are just a few steps away from one of the busiest spots in Paris, the Place Saint-Germain-des-Prés. The Place's large terrace cafés once served as *salons* for legendary writers and artists such as Pablo Picasso, Jean-Paul Sartre, Simone de Beauvoir and Guillaume Appollinaire. Today, many Parisians say that the *salons* of the *rive gauche* have moved to Charlotte Aillaud's residence on the tiny Rue du Dragon. Françoise Sagan, Franco Zeffirelli, Jeanne Moreau and Leonard Bernstein are just a few of the many talented people who meet there regularly in gatherings where the conversation is likely to be as subtle and original as the food, the wine, the music and the surroundings.

Much of the mystique has to do with the way in which Mme Aillaud and her late husband Emile arranged their courtyard, house and garden. Combining their disparate interests, they invented and orchestrated their own design for living. Emile Aillaud was one of France's most distinguished architects, who masterminded La Dé-

Far right, in summer the marble terrace, shaded by a white canvas awning, is used for outdoor dining.

Above right, along one ivy-covered wall and half-hidden behind the feathery, cone-shaped *Taxus baccata*, Charlotte Aillaud sets out pots of rhododendrons and white-flowering gardenias in spring and summer.

Below right, viewed from a first-floor window, the garden appears secluded and calm, the large horse chestnut and sycamore trees affording a welcome, dappled shade.

Previous page left, the swags of ivy draped over the ground-floor windows add to the garden's atmosphere of mystery, which is felt as much within the house as without.

Previous page right, an old provençal terracotta pot contains Mme Aillaud's favourite white roses, while a topiary rabbit hides under some ivy.

fense and the Paris suburb of La Grande Borne. Charlotte Aillaud is a contributing editor to *Architectural Digest* and a regular at some of Europe's most important classical music and opera festivals. She is also a close friend of a number of celebrated writers and directors, including William Faulkner and Joseph Losey.

And she is famous for her garden. The basic design was obviously influenced by her husband's sense of scale and proportion, but Charlotte Aillaud alone is responsible for its disarming, dream-like atmosphere.

Like many private gardens in Paris, this garden was intended as a sort of setting for, and extension to, the ground floor of the house. The *hôtel* was originally built in the seventeenth century, but was altered and enlarged in the mid-nineteenth century. When the Aillauds arrived, the garden was not much more than a mass of ivy and a patch of weeds with large horse chestnut and sycamore trees at the bottom.

As soon as you go through the *hôtel's* carriage entrance, built in 1673, you sense that this garden is special. Beyond the *concierge's* charming lodge, the cobbled courtyard curves invitingly. In the centre

stands a single *Catalpa bignonioides*, the Indian bean tree, which bears beautiful panicles of white and yellow foxglove-like flowers in July, followed by long, slender pods. Four stone steps lead up to the L-shaped house, which borders the eighty-metre garden. Restful, and with a soothing symmetry, it is at the same time full of unorthodox surprises. Practical, decorative and quirky, this is a garden shaped by personality rather than by any formula.

Because the *hôtel*'s main reception rooms all have French windows giving on to the garden, evergreens were essential for garden interest throughout the year. Ivy grows thickly over all the façades and garden walls, and drapes itself like garlands over the windows of the white marble and gilt dining room – designed by Percier and Fontaine – and of the more intimate red salon, furnished in Fortuny covers. Outside, in order to extend the living space into the garden and vice versa, the Aillauds added a white marble terrace, shaded in spring and summer with a simple white canvas awning.

Among the garden's many distinctive fea-

Placed in the centre of the garden, the stone fountain stands on axis with the main entrance to the shadowy area framed by the four feathery yews.

tures, the central focal point is a white stone fountain set on a tall pedestal so that it can be seen from inside the house. The trickling jet of water and the splashing and twittering of birds encourage the sensation of pastoral seclusion. Around the fountain, at the four cardinal points, Mme Aillaud has planted four, two-metre-high cone-shaped yews, *Taxus baccata*, which serve not only to frame the fountain but also, with their impressive height, to break up the space. Though clipped into shape, they are not as severely manicured as in most classic French gardens, and they look particularly soft and delicate when light filters through their new, feathery growths.

When the Aillauds started planting they decided to leave the rich layers of dark green ivy, *Hedera helix*, that had scrambled for decades over the garden walls. But as old ivy vines inevitably have bare, straggly base roots, Charlotte Aillaud decided to camouflage them with a low yew hedge. Clipped into architectural, rectangular shapes, the hedge also marks the junction between the house and the garden. As Mme Aillaud says, 'It is a simple solution to a difficult problem.'

Because conditions in most European city gardens imply poor soil and varying amounts of pollution and light, temperamental plants are usually avoided. Mme Aillaud solved her planting problems by using terracotta and stone pots to protect favourite camellias and gardenias, which she brings to Paris from the garden of her country house near Fontainebleau. More rustic, white-flowering plants, including the dwarf *Astilbe* x *crispa* and *Artemisia lactiflora*, both with long, plume-like flowers from July to September, and a beloved 'Mme Alfred Carrière' rose, with recurrent fragrant blooms flushed with pink, are also put in pots which are wrapped against cracking in the winter.

But above and beyond the thick mantles of ivy, the feathery yews and the soothing

When seen from the far side of one of the box fleur-de-lys, tall rose bushes add both height and striking dashes of colour to a corner of the white marble terrace.

fountain, the true highlights of the garden are revealed. The four fleurs-de-lys in box, *Buxus sempervirens*, stand one in each corner of the garden. They were designed like this for two reasons: to add a note of over-scaled whimsy, and to solve the dilemma of ground cover. Clipped at about thirty centimetres high, the three-metre by three-metre emblems pose elegant riddles of scale and proportion, suddenly bringing the space to life. The juxtapositioning of tall, conical yews and low box fleurs-de-lys is an example of a phenomenon more usually associated with large parterres in gardens on a grand scale. Thus, it is as if Charlotte Aillaud had arranged elements of a country château in her intimate Parisian garden.

The special atmosphere of this garden is the result of a unique combination of a traditional French approach to garden principles and plant materials combined with a sense of caprice and a taste for natural-looking growth. Nothing is strictly polished, yet nothing is left to grow wild. There is a pleasing, ethereal quality much like that of the dream sequence in Jean Cocteau's *La Belle et la Bête*. In this garden, the line between reality and fantasy disappears. The big, noisy world of Paris is only a few seconds away, but Charlotte Aillaud's garden is a secluded refuge, a privileged place for family, friends and reveries.

12

A HERB
AND ROSE GARDEN

VIIe arrondissement

An aura of privilege lingers over the Faubourg Saint-Germain, where many fine old gardens lie concealed behind centuries-old façades. Never subject to the whimsical vagaries of fashion, the *VIIe arrondissement* has remained discreetly fashionable for over three hundred years. Built on land that until the end of the sixteenth century was open meadows and marshy fields, the 'noble faubourg' still retains many of its historic buildings, and the Rue de l'Université is one of its most characteristic streets. Off it lies this garden, unique in its particular charm,

yet in other ways so typical of the gardens of the district, hidden from all who are not privileged to penetrate behind the great *porte-cochère*, across the cobbled *cour d'honneur*, and through the central block of the *hôtel particulier*.

The history of the area of Saint-Germain goes back to the sixth century, when a small village sprang up around the new basilica of Saint-Vincent and Sainte-Croix, south-west of the city centre. Richly decorated with mosaics, with its dome roofed in copper, the church was pillaged on numerous occasions

Beds planted with roses were laid beside the path that borders the central lawn.

Previous page left, at the end of one of the house's side wings a door opens onto the secluded garden.

Previous page right, one of the garden's eye-catching features – and a family heirloom – a statue of Cupid made by the mid-eighteenth-century French sculptor Etienne Maurice Falconet.

during the Norman invasions of the ninth century. When Philippe Auguste circled Paris with a defensive wall in the twelfth century, the reconstructed abbey found itself outside the ramparts. Renamed Saint-Germain-des-Prés, after the meadows (*prés*) that swept westward along the banks of the Seine, it now had jurisdiction over a wealthy parish covering most of the area that today constitutes the *V^e* and *VIe arrondissements*. Ten thousand people lived within the confines of the fortified abbey alone.

The meadow lands to the west of the abbey, however, traditionally fell under the jurisdiction of the city's university, a circumstance which gave rise to bitter wrangles between the churchmen of the two camps. Known as the 'Pré-aux-Clercs', the clerics' meadow, the open site had, by the fourteenth century, become a favourite haunt of students, whose right to be there was disputed by the abbey. A legal judgement found in the university's favour, but shortly afterwards a canal was dug right across the meadow to supply water from the Seine to the abbey's defensive moats. By 1540 this was deemed redundant and filled in, which finally permitted expansion on the western edge of the *rive gauche*.

At this point the story of the *faubourg* crosses the river to the Marais, the centre of aristocratic Parisian life in the early seventeenth century and home to one of the most amorous figures in French history, Marguérite de Valois, daughter of Catherine de Médicis and Henri II. Popularly known as 'la reine Margot', the childless Queen lived in the Hôtel de Sens after her separation from her husband Henri IV, who went on to marry Marie de Médicis. After the murder of one of Queen Margot's paramours by a jealous rival, who in his turn was beheaded, the Queen left the *rive gauche* in 1606, determined to build a palace on the river bank opposite her mother's Tuileries, on the site of the Pré-aux-Clercs.

Lying perpendicular to the river, Queen Margot's palace was composed according to the same general plan as her mother's, with a central domed pavilion flanked by side wings terminating in end pavilions, one of which overlooked the Seine. Again, as at the Tuileries, two vast gardens extended westwards along the river. A raised terrace gave on to a walled garden containing the Queen's private enclosure, where she constructed a circular domed temple dedicated to Jacob. An already existing street, now known as Rue des Saint Pères, bisected the property, and the second garden lay on the other side of it. Queen Margot planted it with straight avenues of trees – stretching as far as the present-day Assemblé Nationale – box parterres and a shady allée, all of which were open to the public. Margot's avenue inspired her successor Marie de Médicis to construct, in 1616, the Cours la Reine, running from the far end of the Tuileries to distant Chaillot.

On Queen Margot's death in 1615, Louis XIII inherited the palace, along with a mountain of royal debts. Eight years later he sold the vast property to a group of investors, who subdivided the estate and began the great land speculation that soon saw Queen Margot's gardens covered with building works.

At the same time French architects working for the nobility had developed a standard formula – gracious, symmetrical and easy to reproduce – for the great numbers of buildings – from royal palaces to their reduced versions, *hôtels particuliers* – then being constructed in some haste. The Palais du Luxembourg, built on the *rive gauche* for Marie de Médicis just seven years after Queen Margot's palace, reflects the new style. The main or central block, which had previously been flush with the street, was pulled back into the depths of the property and separated from the thoroughfare by a courtyard. Flanking wings ran from the street to join the central core perpendicularly at either side, enclosing the courtyard and containing stabling below and

rooms for domestic staff above. Laid out behind the central block was the garden, reserved for those privileged to have access to the palace or *hôtel particulier*. As such buildings required large, regularly shaped sites, which the crooked medieval streets of the Marais rarely provided, many of the aristocrats and rising bourgeois crossed the Seine, in the wake of Marie de Médicis and Queen Margot, to construct the residences now regarded as masterpieces of French seventeenth- and eighteenth-century architecture.

The garden on the Rue de l'Université, though radically transformed, can trace its history right back to the district's earliest days in the mid-seventeenth century. In 1639, just ten years after Louis XIII's

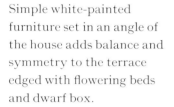

Simple white-painted furniture set in an angle of the house adds balance and symmetry to the terrace edged with flowering beds and dwarf box.

decision to sell up, Pierre Pitou, Councillor of the High Court in Paris, bought his plot of land. Six years later he began the construction of a typical *hôtel particulier*, with a courtyard, side wings and a garden concealed behind the central block. He leased it to a fellow councillor, Michel Barberie, in 1671, who in turn drew up a contract with Jean Hotot, a local gardener. This spelt out his duties, which were, among other things, to ' . . . cultivate the land, to supply and lay manure, to prune the grape vines and fruit trees and look after them properly, to sow in the said garden a quantity of seeds, so as to be able to gather all sorts of pot-herbs and salads according to the four seasons, and also to plant all kinds of flowers . . . enclose the said garden and maintain it well kept and watered from time to time when needed, and to return the said garden at the end of the present contract in the state it is currently in . . .'

Sixty years later, the *hôtel*, which was now in the ownership of Pierre Pitou's son, the Marquis de Courcy, another councillor, was leased to the Russian ambassador, Prince Basile Dolgorouski, and transformed into a lavish official residence. The Prince's stay lasted for only a year, but his departure was marked by one of the most brilliant fêtes that the house – or Paris – had ever seen. Three days of festivities culminated in a grand ball held in the garden.

We can guess what the garden looked like at that time to some extent from a brief reference in a contract of sale drawn up in 1737 to a garden flanked by trellis walls. It is clearly marked on the bird's-eye-view map of Paris known as the 'Plan Turbigo' published two years later, which shows a central rectangular *parterre de broderie* of arabesques in box surrounded by a perimeter path. This design, so typical of its time, would have replaced the rustic kitchen garden that would originally have been attached to the house.

Confiscated during the Revolution and

emptied of its contents, the *hôtel* was sold off in 1796, and a map drawn twelve years later indicates, if only faintly, the changes that ensued. Following the contemporary taste for simplicity, the garden was filled with rows of trees, which must have produced the effect of a miniature fort. By the late nineteenth century and well into the twentieth, the garden was laid out with oval

raked beds planted with vivid bedding schemes composed of lurid combinations of flowers and variegated shrubs such as begonias, coleus and *Ageratum mexicanum*.

Today the garden's design reflects the preference of the current occupants – direct descendants of the family who have lived here since the early nineteenth century – for greenery and symmetry, strong colour and form. Within the large four-hundred-square-metre plot they laid a broad lawn with a path marking the central axis. The path is wider at its near end than at the far end, an optical illusion which seems to exaggerate its length, thus creating a sense of greater depth. To increase the illusion, a yew hedge was planted at the far end curving towards the vanishing point, and on it, against the neigh-

Far left, garden furniture is laid out at one end of the gravel path that cuts through the lawn and leads to the leafy enclosure at the opposite end. To give a sense of greater depth the path narrows deliberately towards the far end.

Left, contrasting with the openness of the rest of the garden, a bench and table shaded by a dark green trellis offer a secluded seating area.

With its formal, simple lines the garden complements the classical features of the house.

bouring ivy-covered stone wall, was set a small stone urn.

Flanking the *hôtel*'s enfilade of salons, a narrow terrace runs the length of the central block. Two large clipped evergreen mounds, one of rosemary and the other of lavender, placed on axis with the path, mark the entrance into the garden from the *hôtel*. Planted against the low terrace ledge is an assortment of herbs – mint, sage and basil – a small gesture which, travelling back over the

centuries, recalls the time when the garden was planted with 'all sorts of pot-herbs'.

In a far corner, in the shade of a sycamore, deep pink camellias, planted over twenty-five years ago, now provide vivid spots of colour in late winter, and a *Viburnum tinus* is covered with its metallic-blue berries by the time the mid-spring-flowering pale pink rhododendrons come into bloom.

A quiet corner behind the yew hedge is simply planted with light-reflecting, variegated evergreens, *Euonymus japonicus* 'President Gauthier', and a billowing spotted laurel, which frame a mid-nineteenth-century neo-Gothic iron bench.

Along one of the *hôtel*'s two side wings is a secluded rose walk, which in summer makes a colourful screen. Rising within a border of dwarf box, *Buxus sempervirens* 'Suffruticosa', is a collection of roses which fill the otherwise green garden with their brilliant reds, yellows and pinks during the summer months. The popular Victorian Hybrid perpetual 'Baroness Rothschild', with fragrant rose-pink cup-shaped flowers, blooms intermittently with the large, canary-yellow flowers of 'Mme A. Meilland', while the fragrant wine-coloured petals of 'Papa Meilland' contrast with the silvery-pink 'Queen Elizabeth'. Although it is hard to grow in this semi-shaded spot, the much-loved favourite 'Virgo' easily repays the effort, its pure white blooms adding a touch of coolness and echoing the all-white pelargoniums and impatiens that cascade from the Médicis vases placed along the terrace and first-floor balconies.

Opposite the rose bed and against the wall of the side wing are a series of beds edged with small-leafed box. One contains a massive group of chrysanthemums, which by late summer have grown over a metre tall and bloom late into the autumn, and beyond this, along the path, two more beds are planted with low mounds of variegated *Euonymus fortunei* 'Emerald Gold', which contrasts softly with the deep green box. Miniature topiary obelisks in box flank the beds like book-ends, containing the undulating euonymus and emphasizing the classical lines of the whitewashed façades behind.

In the shade of two horse chestnut trees, pruned annually, sits the garden's ode to the mid-eighteenth century: a white marble statue of a cupid drawing a love dart. This is an Italian reproduction of the celebrated statue by Madame de Pompadour's favourite, the sculpture Etienne Maurice

Falconet, who produced many other statues in the genre, including the famous series of cupids known as 'Les Enfants de Falconet'.

Suffused as it generally is with an ethereal pale light, and steeped in its own rich history, this quietly dignified garden encourages a mood of speculation, in which one's thoughts seem inevitably drawn back over the years, and through the many changes, to the calm that must surely have reigned in Queen Margot's shady *allée*.

The garden's restful simplicity can be best appreciated from the seating area shaded by rosebeds.

13

A HILLTOP GARDEN

Mme Saint-Saëns
XVIIe arrondissement

Set in the crowded heart of old Montmartre, behind an unassuming eighteenth-century façade on the steep, cobbled Rue Cortot, in the *XVIIe arrondissement*, Madeleine Saint-Saëns' broad expanse of lawn stretches sleekly towards the horizon, where, uninterrupted, it meets the sky. Quiet and dignified, it occupies an unusually large site on the northern slope of the Butte (the name, literally meaning 'hill', by which Parisians know the area), and virtually next door to the Sacré Coeur and the terraces of Montmartre's famous vineyard. Surrounded as it is by busy streets thronged with tourists virtually throughout the year, the garden retains an extraordinary quality of stillness and calm.

'In the early evening when the trees are veiled in mist, the garden takes on the qualities of a Magritte painting, elusive and surreal,' explains Mme Saint-Saëns. The famous filtered light of Montmartre that suffuses her garden also caught the imagination of the artists who colonized the area from the early nineteenth century. Among them was Renoir, who from 1875 lived and

worked only a few doors down from here, and is said to have painted in this garden. The house he lived in, one of the oldest *hôtels particuliers* on the hill, dating from the mid-seventeenth century, was subsequently rented by many other artists and writers, Emile Bernard, Suzanne Valadon and her son Maurice Utrillo, who painted perhaps the most famous images of old Montmartre. In 1959 it was bought by the city of Paris, and it now houses the Musée du Vieux Montmartre.

When Mme Saint-Saëns and her late husband first visited the hilltop house to rent in 1948 they found both the aged interiors and the garden plot in a terribly dilapidated condition. 'The previous tenants had over fifty cats which ran wild in the place. So many of the original boiseries were damaged beyond repair that, much to our regret, we had to remove them. The garden, which we were told was over a hectare in area, was a cats' paradise, full of weeds running rampant, with decaying branches lying where they had fallen among the undergrowth. It seemed to cast a spell over the house, and also over us. We were enchanted,' Mme Saint-Saëns recalls.

In order to preserve the character of the street, lined with the low, ochre-washed façades so typical of the old village of Montmartre, the large, three-storey house had been bought by the city of Paris. The municipality had already, in 1933, undertaken perhaps the most imaginative scheme to protect the area, when it created an enclosed, terraced vineyard next to the Museum and the garden that was to belong to the Saint-Saëns. Over three thousand grapevines were planted as a symbolic gesture towards safeguarding the village atmosphere, then threatened by building work, and towards recapturing the agricultural heritage of the steep hillside, which historically was cultivated by the nuns of the Dames de Montmartre abbey. Founded in 1622, the order owned and maintained the

majority of the Montmartre vineyards until after the Revolution when, in 1794, the abbey was disbanded and its lands parcelled up and sold off. At the time when it was annexed to the city of Paris in 1860, Montmartre was dotted with modest houses and carefully tended gardens, which gradually disappeared towards the end of the nineteenth century as the city expanded northwards and land speculation increased.

Now the Butte is carefully guarded by the local authority and residents, whose major concern is the massive annual influx of tourists, who flock by their thousands to the Sacré Coeur. All this activity passes by unnoticed, however, in Mme Saint-Saëns' garden, apparently set so peacefully in a placid country landscape.

Perched high on the hill's northern face, the garden's large expanse is divided into two distinct parts, a flat terrace, levelled out of the hillside, and a steeply sloping bank. The contrast between these two areas is one of the factors which makes this garden so unusual. From the whitewashed neoclassical garden façade there stretches a vast thirty-by-forty-metre level plane, flanked on either side by low stone party walls almost hidden by the dense foliage of neighbouring trees. Beyond, at the far end from the house, the land regains its natural profile and drops sharply to the street below. From Mme Saint-Saëns' windows this bank performs the same function as the eighteenth-century ha-ha, allowing the eye to travel uninterrupted across the terrace to the distant horizon, thereby creating an illusion of limitless space.

'We wanted to keep the garden very simple, without intricate divisions or rare plantings, so as to enhance its enormous size,' says Mme Saint-Saëns. After the initial laborious clearing of the undergrowth from the levelled area, she and a neighbour planted two privet hedges running parallel with each other from the corner of the house to the end of the terrace, a distance of some

Opposite, on the hill at the end of the garden, surrounded by wooded shade and with dense ivy underfoot, lie low benches – a cool retreat at the height of summer.

Previous page left, in one corner of Madeleine Saint-Saëns' garden is a bed full of hydrangeas, from which the lawn stretches into the distance interrupted only by the centrally placed pool covered in water lilies.

Previous page right, reflected in the cool pond, the whitewashed façade of the house is slowly being engulfed in Virginia creeper.

Against a backdrop of trees and tall lilac bushes, the garden's far reaches are planted with two beds, one full of rhododendrons and hydrangeas, the other bursting with rose bushes.

thirty-five metres. Dividing the space into three long rectangles, the clipped hedges emphasize the garden's impressive length and exaggerate the sense of perspective. Their geometry is enhanced by an already existing procession of Norway maples, *Acer platanoides*. Planted at regular intervals along the stone walls behind the metre-high hedges, they make a framework of dappled green foliage, turning yellow in autumn. Six recently planted oriental cherries, *Prunus serrulata* 'Seiboldii', break the symmetry and disturb the tunnel-like impression, standing directly behind the hedge on the left side, where they form a soft cloud of double pink blossoms in early May.

The entire terrace is covered with a green carpet of grass, which imposes a uniformity and harmony on the garden's sections when viewed from the house. The great expanse of lawn is punctuated at the centre by a circular

pool, three and a half metres in diameter, with a wide stone rim lying flush with the grass. Reflected in its glassy surface, along with the open sky is a hummock of elegant water lily leaves. The water lily genus, Nymphaeaceae, is native to almost every country in the world, with species from climates as diverse as Finland (*N. fennica*), Australia (*N. gigantea*) and North America (*N. odorata*), and includes exotic tropical blooms such as the blue lotus of India, (*N. stellata*), and the sacred Egyptian *N. lotus*. The Buddhists of western Asia also endowed it with divine significance, and used it to border the rectangular pools in their garden retreats. Nowadays the most commonly grown water lilies, like those in Mme Saint-Saëns' garden, derive from hybrids developed by the French breeder Latour-Marliac in the late nineteenth century. By crossing the hardy native European species, notably *N. alba*, with the more delicate and exotic tropical ones he led the way to the development of the fifty or more hardy, colourful varieties available today, which, without having lost any of their luxuriant exoticism, are adaptable to virtually any temperate conditions. Here, with their delicate cup-shaped blooms, white flushed with pink, and shapely, glossy leaves, they add to the garden's peaceful, rural charm.

Beyond the pool framed by the privet hedges and tall maples, two curved flowerbeds delineate the far end of the terrace. Here, in a collection of flowering shrubs and perennials, is the garden's concentration of brilliant colour, drawing the eye to the far reaches of the terrace and the distant horizon. Lilac bushes, *Syringa vulgaris*, form a dense leafy backdrop, closing off the end of the terrace without blocking the view.

Massed underneath the lilacs are a wide variety of spring bulbs, including tulips in vivid shades of yellow, red and pink; blue and purple hyacinths; mauve crocuses; yellow daffodils and pure white snowdrops. Seen from the house they form blocks of strong pigments, chosen deliberately to brighten up the view in the grey days of spring, which seem to merge into an impressionistic kaleidoscope of colour.

As spring's cold light gives way to the warmer radiance of summer, the palette of colours in the far beds becomes correspondingly more muted. By mid-June, when the lawn is suffused with the softly filtered light that seems to be unique to Paris, the bulbs have been replaced by soft-toned Floribunda roses. Derived from crosses of dwarf Polyanthas and Hybrid Teas, the modern Floribunda varieties have become increasingly popular for their great hardiness, resistance to disease and wide range of colours. In Mme Saint-Saëns' garden double 'Iceberg' blooms provide pure white accents for yellow and pink varieties, including the scented light pink 'Poulsen's Pearl' and mid-yellow 'Sun Flare'.

To the left of the semicircular rose bed, in the far corner between the lilac bushes and the hedge, a curved plot contains a group of common flowering shrubs which add further colour. Mulched annually to keep the soil cool and retain moisture in summer while feeding the plants' roots, this bed contains acid-loving plants, which thrive in the open location. In May the large, bell-shaped yellow blossoms of the rhododendron hybrid 'Crest' bridge the flowering seasons of the bottom beds, as do clusters of peonies, *Paeonia officinalis*, which border the bed, including the deep pink double 'Rosea plena' and white 'Alba plena'. In late summer these are replaced with pink hydrangeas, turning to rusty brown in autumn.

In the heat of summer the strips of lawn to either side of the central section become cool, refreshing walks. At the far edge of the terrace they end in low stone benches, which mark the land's sharp descent and are virtually engulfed in the sea of dark ivy which covers the steep bank. A narrow path cut through the dense evergreen ground cover winds down through a thicket of sycamores and *Robinia pseudoacacia* and climbs back up the other side. Further down in the woods the city of Paris has created a nature reserve to protect the hillside's natural flora which would otherwise have disappeared from the urban landscape.

Thus Madeleine Saint-Saëns' garden is a haven not only for its owner but also for a part of Montmartre's rural past; a reminder of the time when the Butte sheltered only a small village, as well as a coolly restrained retreat from the busy streets of present-day Montmartre. She, too, was surprised to discover it: 'Over forty years ago the notion of living in Montmartre had never even crossed my mind, nor did I imagine that there could be such a peaceful spot within the city's boundaries. To have come across this house and the garden was a stroke of good fortune, and I wouldn't exchange them for anything in the world.'

14

THE ELEPHANT GARDEN

Baroness Lulu de Waldner
VIIe arrondissement

When the Baroness de Waldner rented the Hôtel de Maillebois, there was one condition: that she be responsible for creating a garden on the tract of land behind the historic *hôtel particulier*. The august financial institution that owns the building might now be surprised to see the extent of the return on their investment. In just over a decade, Lulu de Waldner has transformed this large square plot in the Faubourg Saint-Germain into a garden that must rank among the most enchanting in Paris.

Over the past decade, this ingenious gardener has also been responsible for creating a most striking garden at Jas Créma, in the harsh and arid landscape of Haute Provence. Her love of gardens goes back even further: her garden at Mortefontaine on the Île de France is justly remembered for its exquisite planting. Some of her ideas have now become known as the hallmarks of the Waldner style. The colourful combinations of strawberries, lettuce, pansies and sweet williams spilling over lavender-edged chequerboard squares at Mortefontaine became legendary; the menagerie of topiary animals dotted

around the grounds – clipped yew horses' heads poking out of hedges near stables and swans near the water's edge – inspired many imitations; and a heady combination of Banksian roses, wisteria and clematis clambering into the branches of fruit trees was a Waldner favourite. Baroness de Waldner cultivated the garden at Mortefontaine for over thirty years, until the day her lease was not renewed, when she was compelled to look elsewhere.

In 1978, having accepted the stipulation laid down by the Hôtel de Maillebois' owners, she set to work on the large plot, nearly twenty-five metres square. Set back from one of the principal thoroughfares of the Faubourg Saint-Germain, on the Rue de Grenelle, the *hôtel*, built by Louis XIV's chief architect Antoine Le Pautre, dates back to the mid-seventeenth century. Le Pautre is also credited with the exceptional Hôtel de Beauvais in the Marais quarter, with its oval courtyard and famous suspended terrace gardens. He designed the Hôtel de Maillebois with a monumental arched entrance, leading to a magnificent building with two wings flanking a central block that gave out onto a

vast garden that extended as far as the Rue Saint-Dominique. The size of the garden was drastically reduced in the nineteenth century, when the Boulevard Saint-Germain was cut through the area.

Always the home of high-ranking clergy and noblemen, the *hôtel* was rented in 1750 to the ageing Duc de Saint-Simon, who finished his famous *Mémoires* and died there in 1755.

In 1783, Jacques-Denis Antoine, the architect responsible for the Hôtel des Monnaies, the French mint, was engaged by the Comte de Maillebois to renovate the central section of the *hôtel* for his young son. Antoine detached the central block and pushed it back into the garden space, creating an unusually large courtyard, now cobbled in granite with a central circular lawn. The courtyard façade, in the neoclassical style with pilasters rising through three storeys to support ornate stone urns, is in great contrast with the garden façade. Simple and more modest, this is in a style that can be seen in late eighteenth-century provincial houses throughout France.

Unlike so many gardens, where the house seems to extend beyond its walls, here the garden carries its influence up the white

Previous page left, leading from the flower-filled salons, the wide stone terrace is flanked on either side with pink-flowering camellias. Terracotta pots planted for spring bloom with white tulips.

Previous page right, detail of the filigree iron garden bench positioned in the shade against a bank of spreading creeper.

Left, the garden is protected from bustling city life by high walls and tall trees, with only distant glimpses of neighbouring buildings.

Below, looking down the length of the garden, the central feature, Baroness de Waldner's topiary elephant, can be viewed to greatest effect.

Framed by the clipped box, the elephant grazes in a bed of cotoneaster and spring-flowering narcissi.

stone steps, across the semicircular terrace and into the house, leaving its mark throughout. The house is full of the evidence of Lulu de Waldner's life-long passion for flowers. Framed botanical prints and small still lifes hang on the salon walls; fabrics in floral patterns are everywhere; and every surface has a delicate vase of cut flowers from the garden. Ladybirds, indispensable in any garden and a Waldner talisman, decorate needlepoint cushions, wallpapers and even the telephones.

Outside the French windows that lead from the salon to the terrace is an assortment of watering cans poised waiting for use. Lulu de Waldner is not only single-handedly responsible for the layout and planting scheme of the garden, but she is also its sole daily labourer. With occasional help from one man who cuts the grass and another who expertly clips the box topiary, she is more often than not to be found half-hidden among the foliage, staking or dead-heading the roses.

A wide stone terrace curves out into the garden space, flanked at either end by a huge *Camellia japonica*. In early spring, the glossy evergreen leaves are almost obscured by the large crimson double flowers. Weathered terracotta pots decorated with swags and animal heads are planted with creamy-white tulips, placed near the French windows so as to frame the views from within.

Later in the summer *Clematis montana*, also grown in terracotta pots, smothers its iron topiary supports with flowers. 'It is always very important to add height in a

garden', explains Baroness de Waldner. 'So often everything in this country is planted flat.' The clematis trained over the iron sphere is an example of the non-traditional plant materials she employs in order to create a sense of fantasy, while at the same time providing the necessary height.

Another example of her use of topiary, impossible to overlook, stands at the far end of the garden: a life-size young elephant in clipped box, grazing in the middle of a low, oval-shaped mound of evergreen *Cotoneaster dammeri*. In spring it stands knee-deep in pure white *Narcissus triandrus* 'Alba', and in autumn it seems to be standing in a scarlet sea of cotoneaster berries, a favourite of the birds. The elephant is not alone: its pair, festooned each spring with yellow Banksian roses, stands in a sea of lavender at Jas Créma.

Behind the Parisian elephant is a bank of *Arundinaria viridistriata*, the striped Japanese bamboo. Its yellow-green spring foliage, turning darker in autumn, provides a contrasting background against which the elephant's silhouettte stands out sharply. A metre-high box hedge surrounds the elephant, which dominates the garden's central sweeping expanse of lawn. Six domes of box, three on either side, run the length of the hedge, and complete the planting in this central area.

Bordering the central area are two rectangular gardens. On one side, hidden under a canopy of horse chestnut trees, is the shady garden. Winding through it from the edge of the terrace is a narrow serpentine path, its outline subtly suggested in spring by occasional clusters of white narcissi among the grass. This woodland walk meanders through naturalized plantings which seem to increase the scale of the plot as well as providing delightful surprises among the tall trees. Clusters of creamy lenten roses, *Helleborus orientalis*, bloom in early spring, giving way in summer to clumps of *Hosta plantaginea*, with heart-shaped leaves and racemes

of fragrant white flowers.

Further along the winding path, beyond a *Mahonia japonica*, which turns bronze in autumn and scents the air with its vivid yellow flowers in winter, are some *Camellia japonica* 'Imura', newly planted against the ivy-covered stone wall. In spring the single white flowers seem to float in the dark green space, creating ghostly highlights against the dark blue-green holly hedge at the bottom of the path. Concealed behind this is one of Baroness de Waldner's secrets of good gardening: two rich compost heaps.

On the opposite side of the garden, balancing the shady area, is a narrow plot overflowing with flower and foliage growth. Sheltered by a three-storey stone wall, this south-facing garden receives full sun all day. Here, in what Baroness de Waldner dismisses as 'an over-planted mess', is a romantic tangle of soft-coloured roses and climbers with

Opposite, the formal, box bushes planted around the edges of the lawn contrast sharply with the rampant growth of the garden's climbing roses.

At the far end of the garden lies a secluded grass corner bordered by a cascade of Philadelphus 'Virginal', which creates a highly scented backdrop. In the middle rises an abstract topiary form shrouded in variegated ivy.

variegated leaves, twining into each other at will.

Dividing this garden from the central area, and planted directly behind the box hedge, is a spreading honey locust tree, *Gleditsia triacanthos* 'Sunburst'. Its bright golden foliage stands out against the soft grey-green leaves of the dwarf *Pyrus salicifolia* 'Pendula' planted next to it. Along the edge of the path is a spreading carpet of pink lilies of the valley, *Convallaria majalis* 'Rosea', one of the many plants transplanted from the garden at Mortefontaine.

At the foot of the wall is a curved bed containing a number of old-fashioned roses, including the apricot-coloured Hybrid musk 'Buff Beauty' and 'Mabel Morrison', underplanted with billowing evergreen *Euonymus*

The woodland walk that runs down one side of the lawn is full of some of Baroness de Waldner's favourite plants – camellias, mahonia, hellebores and blue-tinged ilex.

Terracotta pots and seats decorated with elephants are distributed around the terrace. Beyond is the entrance to the perfumed side garden full of roses.

fortunei 'Kewensis', which gives year-round ground cover.

Cascading down the high stone wall are the fragile white, sweetly scented clusters of the Banksian rose, *R. banksiae*. Its prolific growth completely covers the wall, and its canes cast arching shadows on the grass path below. Further down the garden are recurrent, velvety red blooms of the vigorous climber 'Etoile de Hollande' which sway gently against the sky.

At the far end of the winding path is a sheltered garden seat, with tendrils of *Vinca major* poking through its graceful wrought-iron arabesques. On the circular grass area in front of it, a strange twisted form swathed in variegated ivy marks the end of the path.

The ivy has been allowed to run rampant since the half-hardy jasmine with which it used to be mingled died in a recent cold winter. Forming a towering backdrop to the garden and framing the seat is a *Philadelphus* 'Virginal', laden with orange blossom-scented double white flowers in June and July. Screening the next-door garden, it also creates a secret garden-within-a-garden. Veiled in the soft pinks, creamy yellows, and white of flowering shrubs against foliage in shades of grey, gold and green, this area possesses its own special atmosphere. Here and throughout the garden the Waldner combination of inspiration and intuition has produced qualities which, despite their many imitators, remain inimitable.

15

A Rooftop
Vegetable Garden

M. Christian Duc
IVe arrondissement

Christian Duc's highly individual rooftop garden, suspended above the popular Beaubourg district, can be reached by one of two equally precarious routes: either up a narrow, rickety flight of wooden attic stairs, or from the designer's small kitchen terrace by way of a tall, uncertain-looking metal ladder. But the surprise the visitor receives on first reaching this unorthodox garden handsomely repays the effort of getting there. Every year M. Duc, with the aid of professionals such as the landscape designer Pascal Cribier, transforms his roof into an

idiosyncratic garden and platform for the spectacular views of the Paris skyline. From its position six storeys up in the heart of the *IVe arrondissement*, practically on top of the Pompidou Centre, the windswept site commands panoramic views of the city's innumerable domes, steeples and monuments, receding to the distant horizon through almost 360 degrees.

The 1940s apartment block stands on the Rue du Renard in the Marais, so called after the marshland which once filled the area, and which was drained by the religious foun-

The whimsical nature of the garden is seen best from a neighbouring rooftop. Below centre, the kitchen terrace's jungle-like atmosphere contrasts with the unexpectedly spacious plot above; the steep ladder between the two is shrouded in cascading, heavily scented honeysuckle.

dations who settled here in the thirteenth century. By that time the Marais was already included within the city boundaries, as defined by the fortified walls with over a dozen crenellated gatehouses built by Philippe Auguste in the twelfth century. By the sixteenth century the area had become fashionable, and a maze of narrow, twisting streets lined with tightly packed houses had sprung up, as can be seen in the Truchet or 'Bale' map of the city, published in 1551. By the mid-nineteenth century the population had swelled massively, but continued to be served by only the most rudimentary sanitation system. The severe public health problems that inevitably ensued prompted Baron Georges Haussmann, appointed *Préfet* of the Seine *département* by Napolean III, to drive a network of wide axial avenues and straight boulevards, such as the boulevard Turbigo in 1854, and a year later the neighbouring Boulevard Sébastopol, through the cramped medieval and renaissance streets. The Rue du Renard, with its northern cont-

inuation the Rue Beaubourg, was built in 1868 as one of the main arteries from the north-east to the south of the city. Over the last twenty years the district has seen considerable changes, including the controversial transfer of Les Halles, the city's famous food markets, to the suburbs, to be replaced by a shopping centre, and the construction of the Pompidou Centre, which draws streams of visitors to what has become one of the liveliest areas in Paris. Few would suspect the existence of Christian Duc's garden, high above it all.

He first cultivated the flat, rectangular roof in 1983. Now every winter, he starts planning his theme for the following year, which he will begin planting out in April. The theme is different every year: 'I find it suits me to start afresh. The excitement of beginning again keeps me alert, which is perhaps why I've never lived in the same place for more than six or seven years. Whenever I do decide to move, the excitement of finding something new outweighs the sadness of

Previous page left, planted afresh every year by M. Duc, the garden at one time was a re-creation in miniature of a Greek island landscape. The current layout, conceived by the landscape designer Pascal Cribier, includes a flourishing *potager*.

Previous page right, cloches are laid out in parallel rows. Planted underneath, vegetables are protected from frost and encouraged into early growth.

leaving a place that has become familiar.' This restless, questing spirit, which is apparent in all Christian Duc's projects, whether for furniture, jewellery, silverware or promoting the work of a forgotten craftsman, governs his approach to his roof-space, where he starts from scratch every year. 'A couple of years ago I was fascinated by the sort of vegetation typical of stark, arid Greek island landscapes, so I planted masses of different sorts of rosemary, lavender and thyme among the sedum that I used as ground cover. It looked extremely striking against the gothic Tour Saint-Jacques in one direction and the funnel-like ventilation shafts of the Beaubourg in the other. Another year I planted dozens and dozens of tall sunflowers, which formed two beautiful horizontal blocks of colour, green below with a vivid streak of yellow above. But it was no fun when the time came to pull them up and burn them in late October', he recalls. The other major reason for treating the space on an annual basis was a practical one: in winter and early spring the unprotected rooftop is whipped by strong winds, and M. Duc had no wish to get involved in elaborate schemes for constructing permanent windbreaks which would have destroyed its open feel. Weight was also a factor, and shrubs and trees in pots were easier to bring inside for the winter.

The garden has now become a joint venture, with Christian Duc finding that his ideas, based on the conceptual and abstract evocation of many different garden styles within the limited area were sympathetically echoed by Pascal Cribier. Based in Paris since he started his own landscape design practice in 1982, Pascal Cribier has worked on projects all over France, from Provence to Chartres, where he is currently transforming the gardens of a château to include tumbling cascades of clematis in the old moat. 'I am always interested in the unexpected or startling in a landscape, like the incredibly lush Mogul gardens I have just visited, lost in the

desolate Rajasthan desert', he says. For him the rooftop seemed to present the perfect opportunity for creating a series of subtle visual references to larger, more established gardens.

The steep metal ladder that climbs up from the small shady terrace off the kitchen, planted with a jungle of hostas, day lilies and evergreen ferns, is engulfed in an avalanche of honeysuckle. Passing a pair of large terracotta pots spilling over with purple-flowering thyme on the way, the astonished visitor discovers, on reaching the rooftop, a thick golden carpet of stonecrop, *Sedum acre*, covering the entire surface. Originally intended for a much smaller area, the matlike evergreen simply took over, and has now spread everywhere. In May and June it turns brilliant yellow as its thousands of flowers open, and tufts of self-sown grass here and there add a rather surreal, pastoral touch.

A U-shaped strip of low mounds of *Lobelia erinus* divides the space into two separate parts. Grown in concealed narrow black plastic troughs, the lobelia forms an extraordinary dwarf purple-blue hedge against the yellow-green sedum, successfully confounding conventional notions of both colour and scale. On one side of it stands a well-drilled row of crisp white pelargoniums in pots, while on the other is the roof's most remarkable feature, the kitchen garden. A further surreal touch is added by a pair of iron chairs by André Dubreil, placed at the

White potted geraniums dot the edge of the rooftop garden. In the distance, the unmistakable form of the Pompidou Centre looms impressively.

The rooftop garden with its ground cover of *Sedum acre*, opening out to views of Paris beyond.

far end, as if to enjoy distant views of the garden, while a symbolic 'entrance', marked by a gap in the lobelia, is shaded by a group of large-leaved deciduous trees as standards, including a pink-flowering lilac. Behind them M. Cribier lined up three serried ranks of dwarf box in pots, in a direct reference to the more usual use of this most traditional of French edging plants. The kitchen garden, enclosed by the box and lobelia, was born of both men's delight in the unexpected; M. Cribier was intrigued by the idea of raising fruit and vegetables at such altitude, while M. Duc was simply enchanted with the idea of harvesting the crops after all the work of weeding and watering was over. Inspiration for M. Cribier came from the antique, purple-tinged glass cloches that M. Duc discovered one day. He immediately saw row upon row of beds, straight as a die, planted with herbs and vegetables laid out with immaculate precision. Now all that remained was to bring the idea to fruition.

Perhaps the supreme example of a walled kitchen garden in France is at Versailles: the vast area of raised beds and espaliered walls, with its own complex irrigation system, designed for Louis XIV by Jean-Baptiste de la Quintinie between 1677 and 1683. The garden's enormous size (eight hectares) and tremendous yield of crops was a reflection of the French court's growing demand for better and more varied fruit and vegetables. By the eighteenth century no major château or country estate in France or the rest of Europe was without its walled garden and army of gardeners to supply increasingly refined aristocratic palettes with fresh produce on a daily basis. Towards the middle of the century heated greenhouses appeared, usually constructed of brick, and warmed by furnaces built against the outside wall, which permitted the cultivation of a range of fruit and vegetables virtually throughout the year. Tropical and subtropical plants brought back from expeditions to the colonies also flourished and were propagated in the artificial heat, leading to the craze for exotic-looking fruit and vegetables which swept Europe in the second half of the century.

Perhaps the most flamboyant example of this is 'The Pineapple', a summerhouse built in 1761 for the Earl of Dunmore on his estate near Falkirk in Scotland. While relatively orthodox in a classical manner at ground level, the first floor develops into a massive and botanically correct stone model of the exotic fruit. Along with such follies, kitchen gardens on a grand scale have now virtually disappeared in the face of rising labour costs. The last vestiges in France are perhaps the small, lovingly tended plots that line country lanes, filled with rows of Brussels sprouts, leeks and lettuce.

In M. Duc's eccentric plot M. Cribier arranged a dozen cloches in three straight rows and planted them with large, bright green heads of cabbage. Next to them he constructed a raised vegetable patch, two metres by six, from recycled wood, and filled it with the rich soil mixture essential for producing tender crops with good flavour. In it he planted unusual fruit, vegetables and herbs: 'Apart from the fact that they are all delicious to eat, I chose the mixture of herbs, vegetables and strawberries for their foliage, and arranged them in rows according to their leaf colour, so that they would create interesting contrasts with each other.' Planted in neat rows are strawberries – which produce fruit as late as September – fennel, tufts of chives, radishes, trailing cucumber vines, lettuce, French tarragon, and 'Dark Opal' sweet basil, with deep purple leaves. By midsummer, when the feathery fennel leaves

tower over the bed, the cucumber vines have sprawled across the sedum and the strawberries are ripe for picking, this small *potager* looks quite at home against the dramatic city roofscape.

To be able to stand above the rooftops and enjoy unobstructed views of Paris's skyline is in itself unusual; to be surrounded at the same time by this unique garden, which – with wit and style – manipulates and challenges our preconceived notions of garden design, is even more unusual. It is a rare experience indeed. One can only wonder what it will be like next April. . . .

Against the rooftop landscape the miniature *potager* produces an abundance of tender crops including chives, radishes, cucumbers and carrots. 'After all that weeding and watering, the greatest delight were the strawberries, which I picked until early October,' says M. Duc.

16

A GARDEN
IN THE CLASSICAL STYLE

M. Jean Feray
I^e arrondissement

On the Rue Cambon, not far from the Ritz Hotel in Paris's *I^e arrondissement*, Jean Feray discovered a dilapidated house surrounded by a wasteland that was once a garden. That was thirty years ago. Today, both the house and garden stand as tribute to Feray's expertise – now retired, he was the principal inspector for the Caisse Nationale des Monuments Historiques et des Sites, the government department devoted to the research, classification and preservation of France's architectural and landscape heritage. Moreover, they are personal state-

ments on classical design: everything from landscaping to structural restoration, from furnishings to colour schemes, from lighting to porcelain, were either designed in, or inspired by seventeenth and eighteenth-century style and taste.

The property was originally a small section of the grand estate built by the Maréchal de Luxembourg in the late 1600s. At the same time the neighbouring palace and estate of the Duc de Vendôme were bought by Jules Hardouin-Mansart, who intended to sell the land in lots. Plans were drawn up by

Above, standing at the far end of the expanse of ivy the statue adds a sense of depth to the area.

Opposite, a whitewashed statue stands against the ivy-covered trellis.

Previous page left, a narrow path leads through the ivy *tapis vert*.

Previous page right, iron chairs and stools are arranged formally against an ivy bank.

one of Louis XIV's ministers to construct a grandiose square as a sort of homage to the King, bounded by state buildings and with a massive statue of the King on horseback at its centre. The money necessary for the venture, however, was not forthcoming, and eventually, in 1698, Louis granted the land to the city of Paris, and Mansart was instructed to draw up plans and take charge of construction work. As the Place Vendôme rose, so did the value of the surrounding land. In 1719, therefore, when the Maréchal de Luxembourg's impressive *hôtel particulier* was demolished, the land was parcelled up and sold for vast profit. The land on which M. Feray's house stands was bought by the French architect Tavennot in 1741. Using

the same skilled artisans and craftsmen who worked on his larger projects, such as royal commissions and Parisian *hôtels particuliers*, Tavennot constructed his own house. True to the style of the Louis XV period, it is beautifully proportioned in its simplicity, elegant in its intimacy and rich in refined detail. Yet it is relatively modest in size and was once described by the French writer and critic, Philippe Jullian, as an 'élégante bourgeoise' – in other words, beautiful but not grandiose. Its distinguishing feature, however, is the large drawing room, with its richly carved wood panelling. The intricate work is attributed to Nicolas Pineau who, after working for Peter the Great at Peterhof, returned to France and became a lead-

ing exponent of the development in French Rococo known as *genre pittoresque*.

During the three hundred years between Tavennot's construction and Jean Feray's purchase, the house was altered beyond all recognition. At one time it was the headquarters of a textile manufacturer, at another, a dental surgery. So it was that, in 1954, M. Feray found the house a shambles and the garden destroyed. While original plans and drawings of the house remained, none were found for the garden, but by using the experience gained from studying historical French sites, M. Feray patiently recreated the logical, symmetrical style of the great landscape artists, and of Le Nôtre in particular.

To begin with, a stone terrace was laid the length of the house overlooking the garden. It is used now as an outdoor salon, but it also serves architecturally as a link between the rectangular garden and the house, delineating yet blending the style of both. Next, M. Feray staked out plant beds to separate the garden from those on either side, as well as from the ten-storey, early twentieth-century building that had been erected at the far end. Since he preferred year-round greenery, he planted evergreen shrubs – osmanthus and viburnums – and filled the bed at the bottom with the rarer, dark-leafed *Aucuba japonica*, richer looking than the yellow-spotted laurel commonly found in public parks, but equally well-suited to poor soil conditions. Other traditional evergreens include yew and box, the different shades of green breaking up what could otherwise have been a dense border in a garden where there was already insufficient light, creating instead an illusion of greater width and depth.

True to Le Nôtre's style, the overall theme and beauty of the garden is the graceful, varying shades of green. The only contrast is provided by two dramatic splashes of white. In July and August *Acanthus mollis*, planted in spots where direct sunlight filters through trees or round neighbouring buildings, sends

Japanese aucubas fill the garden's side beds and border the perimeter path which cuts through the ivy growth.

Just doors away from the Ritz Hotel and behind the Place Vendôme, Jean Feray's mid-eighteenth-century *hôtel particulier* and formal garden lie serenely amid the bustle of the *1ᵉ arrondissement*.

In order to recapture the *hôtel particulier*'s former splendour M. Feray searched for and found period urns and statuary. The stone plinths on which they rest were designed by M. Feray himself, paying precise attention to the scale and proportion of the mid-eighteenth-century façade.

Lying majestically at each side of the *tapis vert* the sphinx emphasize M. Feray's love of symmetry and formal composition.

up its tall bracts of small, tubular flowers; and throughout the year an eighteenth-century terracotta statue of 'Summer', whitewashed by M. Feray and placed at the far end of the plot, acts as a focal point, heightening the garden's sense of perspective.

The sombre wall of the ten-storey building, however, still loomed large. M. Feray erected rectangular panels of dark green wooden trellis, seven metres high, thereby removing an eyesore and also adding an architectural touch that his seventeenth-century predecessors had used before him.

The art of trellising has been used widely in Europe for centuries – one of the earliest known examples, can be seen in the garden frescoes from Livia's Prima Porta villa in Rome, where they appear as low garden fences. In the seventeenth century, they were used as screens. The French built trellis pavilions; trellises provided high borders around paths and mazes; frames up which plants were trained to climb; and camouflage for bare tree trunks. The trellis has always exemplified man's attempt to control nature, and it still does.

A great defender of historical accuracy, M. Feray uses trellises with only horizontal and vertical lines. The more common, diagonal frameworks seen today were seldom used by Le Nôtre and his followers, since such diagonals obscure and confuse the strong lines of perspective that typify a classical landscape.

Once the terrace, walls, borders and trellises were in place all that remained to be filled was the garden's central, rectangular space. In 1957, and in keeping with seventeenth-century tradition, M. Feray created a large *tapis vert* by planting grass. It did not fare well. 'Grass is so ill-suited to Paris and its difficult atmospheric conditions', M. Feray explained. 'So I had to replace it with something else.' Believing crushed gravel to be 'appropriate only for courtyards and large parks and not the limited dimensions of a city garden', yet faced constantly with the problem of poor soil and sparse light, M. Feray eventually planted the bushy, non-climbing ivy *Hedera helix* 'Conglomerata', which over the years has become a true *tapis vert*. Today, the well-clipped ivy rectangle forms a carpet about forty centimetres high, neither flat nor uniform, but softly billowing and undulating, and constantly reflecting the changing light and shade off its glossy dark green leaves.

Classic French gardens were always designed to be appreciated from both inside and outside the house. It is a feature that M. Feray has borne carefully in mind, for on entering the house the first impression is of the calm yet vivid greenery filling the windows, a welcome haven from the bustle of city life only a few metres away.

A rectangular earth and gravel path has been laid around the ivy and hedge maples, *Acer campestre*, have been planted to right and left. Particularly resistant to air pollution, they cast a delicately dappled shade, and their mid-green leaves, downy on the underside, turn a soft yellow in autumn. At the far end of the garden, because he likes the

pale green of their leaves and the erectness of their structure, ideal for screening, M. Feray planted broad-leaved limes, *Tilia platyphyllos* 'Fastigiata'. A very old specimen of Japanese pagoda tree, *Sophora japonica*, rises dramatically from the ivy bed. In September it bears long and elegant racemes of creamy-white flowers, which are followed in sunny years by slender seedpods. Slightly off centre, it breaks the symmetry, yet adds balance to the whole garden.

Finally, there is a pair of eighteenth-century-style sphinxes. Standing at opposite ends of the terrace, they are cast in resin but are painted to resemble stone. These act as the final, majestic symbol of the serene, formal, classical composition of a garden which is marked, too, by a sure, personal touch.

Above, one of the two model sphinx which are cast in resin and painted to resemble stone.

Opposite, as evening falls the garden's statuary is carefully lit to provide striking focal points among the lush green foliage.

17

A THREE-TIERED GARDEN

M. Maurice Rheims
VIIIe arrondissement

Maurice Rheims' fourth-floor apartment is only a stone's throw away from the Place de la Concorde; the view from his terrace garden, however, seems to be one of uninterrupted greenery, stretching over the lawns and shrubberies of neighbouring gardens to the densely planted trees of the Champs-Elysées and the Grand Palais beyond. M. Rheims, a member of the Académie Française and the author of numerous books, including studies of Gauguin, Toulouse-Lautrec and nineteenth-century sculpture, asked the English landscape de-

signer Russell Page to draw up plans for the six-by-seventeen-metre terrace, which, he says, 'was in total disorder, neither arranged nor designed. There wasn't much there, apart from the concrete slabs and a small rectangular plot of grass.' Thus this small terrace, perched above central Paris, reflects some of the most influential theories of garden design expounded by one of the twentieth century's most celebrated landscape architects.

The south-west-facing site has the advantage of overlooking some of the largest and

The patio, designed by Russell Page to act as an outdoor salon, is simply planted with two large *Pieris japonica*.

stateliest gardens in Paris, lying behind the eighteenth-century façades of the Rue du Faubourg Saint-Honoré. Like its counterpart, and former rival in elegance on the left bank, the Faubourg Saint-Germain, the Faubourg Saint-Honoré dates from the early eighteenth century, when the outlying village of La Roule was incorporated into the city of Paris, and a paved street was laid to connect the two. By 1734 a number of large *hôtels particuliers* had sprung up along the southern side of the street, with gardens stretching down to the tree-lined Champs-Elysées, laid out by André Le Nôtre in 1670. In the nineteenth century many of them were torn down and replaced with larger and grander mansion blocks, like the one in which M. Rheims has his apartment, and others were radically altered, so that all that remains of the eighteenth-century building is the street façade. The most famous of these *hôtels* is of course the Palais de l'Elysée. Built for the Comte d'Evreux in 1718, it later

belonged to Louis XV's favourite, Madame de Pompadour, who enlarged the garden by annexing a parcel of land flanking the Champs-Elysées. Subsequent occupants include Napoleon I, Wellington and Napoleon III, and it has been the official residence of the President of the Republic since 1873. Among other splendid gardens sweeping down to the Avenue Gabriel, and overlooked by M. Rheims, are those of the Japanese, British and American embassies. It was this unique view of parterres and shrubberies, lawns and pools, herbaceous borders and winding paths, all set against the dense foliage of the Champs-Elysées, that inspired Russell Page on his initial visit in 1974.

In his book *The Education of a Gardener*, Page stressed the great importance of initially establishing a central theme or basic idea in order to treat a garden space successfully. 'For a theme of some kind, a basic idea is essential. It will set the rhythm of your composition down to its smallest details. The

Previous page left, crisply painted trellis work and white marble tiles reinforce the formal atmosphere of the balcony.

Previous page right, a honeysuckle-covered arch frames the view of the simply planted balcony.

factor which will suggest the theme may well be some predominating element already on the site.' The 'predominant element' here was clearly provided by the dramatic views; accordingly Russell Page set out to design the terrace around them.

He divided the rectangular terrace, bordered on one side by the wing of the L-shaped apartment, into a series of raised levels culminating in a small area planted for seclusion. Each section of the terrace is treated distinctively, with its own range of plants, sculpture and architectural elements, with the result that an exaggerated impression of depth is created.

A balcony runs the length of the

Intent upon maintaining a simple, slightly formal air in the areas nearest the apartment, Russell Page planted the balcony with white-flowering pelargoniums in circular white tubs.

apartment's south-facing rooms, and at one end projects perpendicularly into the garden. Paved with white marble, it simultaneously reflects light into the rooms and adds a shimmering brightness to the exterior, heightened by the surrounding planting. Stark white troughs contain white zonal pelargoniums, their large clusters of flowers sharply outlined against the emerald-green foliage. Climbing up the balcony supports is a Hall's honeysuckle, *Lonicera japonica* 'Halliana', softening the hard edges with its luxuriant growth and scenting the air from June to October with its fragrant flowers. Dark green trellising, adding a geometrical element to the white wall between the tall French windows, is trained with Virginia creeper. The monochromatic theme of the geraniums and creamy honeysuckle flowers is echoed by the pure, enamelled whiteness of camellias, etched against their glossy deep green foliage. The architectural crispness of the troughs and the trellises and the juxtaposition of whites and greens are the keynotes of the formal treatments so characteristic of Russell Page's urban designs.

At one end of the balcony two steps lead up to the first of the terrace's two raised levels. Weathered rectangular terracotta tiles define the space, which is simply treated with two circular white containers. Flanking the large plate-glass windows that border the space and look out over the spectacular views are more containers, planted with towering evergreen *Pieris japonica*. In April they are festooned with racemes of fragrant bell-shaped flowers which, silhouetted against the dark glossy foliage, continue the white theme onto the second level.

This area is used for outdoor entertaining and therefore is sparsely planted, drawing its 'green' feel from plants on the next level and from the canopy of trees stretching to the city skyline. Page thus incorporates the panorama in the terrace's design, employing it as a dramatic device to lure the viewer's gaze towards the horizon. Along the edge of

this level he built a post-and-lintel structure to frame the view, softening the grey concrete with honeysuckle, which twines along the top beam. Smoked-glass panels a metre high were set between the two posts to act as an unobtrusive barrier.

Three more steps then rise to the highest level, which is entirely filled with plants. By raising it as high as possible Page created a greater depth of soil for planting, a major concern for rooftop gardens. To either side of the steps is a compact cushion of 'Hidcote' lavender, flowering deep blue-purple in early summer. Behind, 'Iceberg' roses bear masses of perfect small white blooms. Screening direct views into the area and framing the narrow entrance on one side is a tall Irish yew, *Taxus baccata* 'Fastigiata'. On the other side is an arching *Syringa vulgaris* 'Charles x'.

Above, from the tiled patio outside the apartment the garden is seen at its most secluded. A crab apple tree marks the centre point, all but concealed in spring by a delicate pink-flowering lilac.

Right, the balcony of M. Rheims' apartment, viewed between the lush natural growth of the three-tiered garden.

The contrast between the sombre evergreen of the yew and the frothy pale pink lilac flowers adds to the sense of mystery in this little garden while increasing the impression of greater depth. A turn-of-the-century ceramic and glass bench stands at the garden's focal point; designed by the Art Nouveau ceramicist, André Muller, it is shaded by the spreading branches of a crab apple, *Malus hupehensis*, planted on the same axis. In late spring deep pink buds open to reveal a profusion of delicate white fragrant flowers, barely visible from inside the

apartment, and therefore adding to the air of surprise.

A dense growth of honeysuckle cloaks the metal railing that encloses the garden, and evergreen flowering shrubs encircle the space. In spring the white, star-shaped flowers of the Mexican orange blossom, *Choisya ternata*, mingle their heady fragrance with those of a *Skimmia japonica*. Occasional groups of narcissi or tulips are used to add highlights to shady corners. Page has limited any strong colour notes to the terrace's furthest reaches, where they

A bench post designed by the early twentieth-century artist André Muller can be glimpsed through the thicket of vegetation that conceals each garden level from the next.

gleam brightly among the dark evergreen foliage, which occasionally parts to allow glimpses of the dramatic views beyond.

The progression of the three distinct levels and their relation to the views exemplify Russell Page's belief in a strong framework and composition. Each area, individually designed in accordance with its function, was nevertheless conceived as part of the whole, and all three areas are intended to flow into each other. Of the difficulties imposed by a site where the view is the dominant feature, Page wrote, '. . . it is usually better to try to reduce the width of a view by planting it out so that from the house you can see it only partially. This, if it is possible, is best done by tree-planting of the simplest kind, using only one or two varieties; a few isolated trees and hedges carefully placed quite near the house will be enough to make a frame and foreground. Above all avoid any garden 'design' or any flower colour which might detract from the main theme, which in such a case must be the view. The ground near the house is also part of the frame. It can be grass lawn or a stretch of sand or gravel. The shadow of trees or passing clouds will give it quite enough interest. If there must be flowers they should be close against the house or below a terrace wall so only visible when you turn your back to the view. I would arrange the gardened part of the garden – flowers and shrubs – to the sides or far enough below so that they and the view are not seen at the same time. On such sites, I try always to reinforce the simplicity of the foreground by arranging a stretch of ground as nearly as possible level with the house. A strong horizontal line is essential to establish foreground and background in their correct places and to accent the vertical lines of trees or hedges.'

Here there is a progression from the quietly formal first level, designed to reflect the architectural planes of the building, with sharp contrasts of green and white breaking the severe lines, to the second level, designed

for open-air dining and entertaining. This spacious, uncluttered area, bordered on either side by dense planting, frames the dramatic view. Beyond this, in turn, is the

third area, a secluded, romantic retreat of soft grass, scented roses and flowering shrubs, which could be found in a country garden.

In this small space, seemingly suspended among the canopy of neighbouring trees, Russell Page has created a peaceful and varied space with many of the attributes of a much larger garden. Practical to use and delightful to look at, with a 'room' to suit every mood, it is also a tempting spot in which to linger and contemplate the magnificent view of the western Parisian skyline.

Stone steps lead up to the third level flanked by mounds of lavender and by white-flowering roses positioned to draw the eye up to the garden's far reaches.

18

A SCENTED COURTYARD

Vᵉ arrondissement

Hidden behind high stone walls on the Rue Amyot, one of the labyrinth of streets that ring the summit of the Montagne Sainte-Geneviève, lies a small, secluded retreat from the bustle of the Latin Quarter. Just a few steps away from the Panthéon in the *Vᵉ arrondissement*, a modest courtyard has been transformed into a delightfully scented garden of great charm and originality.

For centuries this area, the highest point on the left bank, has been one of the city's most important centres of spiritual activity.

Not far from this house and garden – constructed on the site of the seventeenth-century convent of Sainte Aure – traces can still be seen of the vast Roman temple complex that surmounted the hill, believed to have been dedicated to Bacchus. A few centuries later the hill was renamed after Paris's patron saint, Geneviève, who miraculously preserved the city from a series of calamities, including a planned attack by Attila the Hun in AD 450. Over the centuries the area became home to a number of religious orders, and in 1253 Robert de

Opposite, in early spring when the forsythia blooms, white-flowering camellias, planted in terracotta pots, brighten up the granite path.

Previous page left, viewed from an upstairs window, the curved granite path leading to the front door winds round to reveal a different view of the garden and house at every step.

Previous page right, at the far end of the garden, surrounded by heavily scented flowers and foliage, a table and wooden chairs provide a peaceful retreat.

Sorbon founded the theological college which was to become celebrated throughout medieval Europe as the Sorbonne. After the Revolution, when the religious orders were banished, the Latin Quarter (so-called because Latin was the *lingua franca* among students of many different nationalities) shed its theological connections but retained its strongly academic character. It still houses the city's chief educational and research institutes.

Its most famous and prominent landmark, however, is the Panthéon, which stands at the highest point on the left bank. Commissioned by Louis xv in 1744 as a thanks offering after his recovery from a near-fatal illness, the church was to have been dedicated to Sainte Geneviève. It was designed by Germain Soufflot, the young protégé of the Marquis de Marigny, Madame de Pompadour's brother, and the King's superintendent of buildings. After nine years of work on the massive foundations, Louis xv finally laid the foundation stone. The backdrop to this ceremony was a life-size *trompe l'oeil* representation of the building's projected façade, complete with imposing portico. In 1780 Soufflot died, supposedly worn out by his critics, who maintained that as the foundations had been laid on top of Roman clay pits the building was certain to subside. Completed in the year the Revolution started, it became after the death of Mirabeau in 1791 a mausoleum for France's most distinguished citizens. During the nineteenth century it was consecrated as a church, but after the death of Victor Hugo in 1885 it was rededicated to its original purpose. Among the great men buried there are Voltaire, Rousseau, Zola and Soufflot himself.

The Panthéon's massive dome dominates the Parisian skyline, and towers over the garden on the Rue Amyot. The square corner plot is bordered on two sides by high walls, and on the other by the two-storey detached whitewashed house, which would not be out of place in a country town, and a stone-built annexe which links it to the street. The compactness of the area is disguised by the dense concentration of burgeoning growth within its four walls. Faced with the limited dimensions of the former courtyard, the owner decided to fill the space with a profusion of plants that are pleasing to more than one sense. The varied collection of aromatic and highly scented plants, many of them unusual and rarely used in combination, produces a richly sensual experience at any time of the year.

From the stone gateway in the street wall a granite-paved path curves diagonally across the garden to the house's shady front entrance. The walk along this path, although brief, is a series of transient impressions, as each flowering shrub and heady fragrance succeeds the last.

Just inside the street entrance, and running the length of the side wall, is a steep rockery of volcanic stone, its contorted crags and crevices planted with evergreen shrubs and spreading plants to create the effect of a grotto. *Phlox stolonifera* creep over the stones along with the semi-evergreen herringbone-patterned branches of *Cotoneaster horizontalis*, which bear masses of red berries in autumn. Tufts of *Daphne cneorum* dot the bank, its bushy evergreen leaves providing colour throughout the year, and its fifteen-centimetre-high rose-pink flowers scenting the air in May and June. *Viburnum carlesii*, planted along the top of the bank, adds its intoxicating fragrance in April and May, its clusters of waxy white flowers, which appear before the rather sombre foliage, giving way to blue-black berries in midsummer. Periwinkle, *Vinca minor* 'Alba', covered in May with miniature white flowers, trails along the stones, weaving in with cascades of silvery-grey *Gypsophila repens*, which bears tiny white flowers from June to August. At the far end of the rockery, next to the house, a graceful grey birch, *Betula populifolia*, shades the curving

The path through the garden is lined with potted plants and shrubs, including Hinoki cyprus, white-flowering camellias and rhododendrons.

path. Meandering along the wall behind the rockery and engulfing the gateway to the street are twisting vines of honeysuckle, putting the final touch to this carefully contrived chaos of creeping, climbing and trailing plants.

In the curved bed bordering the other side of the path tall, arched clumps of variegated hedge bamboo, *Bambusa multiplex* 'Alphonse Karr' conceal the street entrance from the house, thus creating an illusion of greater depth when viewed from inside the house. Set into the perimeter wall and half-hidden among the fresh green-and-yellow striped bamboo foliage is a Portuguese fountain, constructed from the blue-patterned tiles, or *azulejos*, which are such a common feature in Spanish and Portuguese gardens. Introduced by the Moors in the eighth century, the glazed tiles in muted shades of blue were used both inside houses and outside, where their cool, reflective qualities, especially when associated with water, provided welcome relief from the Mediterranean sun. Used to line pools and fountains and on

pergolas, garden seats and pavilions, the tiles often carried painted scenes, such as the famous panels at the Marquez de Fronteira's seventeenth-century garden at Benfica, or the allegorical scenes on the fountains in the eighteenth-century garden at Quelez, outside Lisbon. *Azulejos* can also be found across the Mediterranean in Naples, where the gardens in the cloister at Santa Chiara are laid out in a geometric pattern of beds and seats decorated with tiles painted with garlands of fruit and flowers.

In this Parisian garden the nineteenth-century tiled fountain, with its chubby putti supporting a carved basin in the form of a shell, adds a touch of fantasy to the stone wall covered in honeysuckle. It rises from mounds of dark-leaved *Skimmia japonica* planted around its base. In early summer the shade-loving shrubs produce panicles of strongly scented white star-shaped flowers, followed by bright red berries in late summer. A spreading *Magnolia grandiflora* bears its spectacularly large and fragrant tulip-shaped flowers in late summer, supplementing the white theme of the garden.

The evergreen shrubs are underplanted with scatterings of *Primula veris*, whose delicate yellow flowers scent the air in May; and from July to mid-October, old-fashioned mignonettes, *Reseda odorata*, bloom in the partial shade. This favourite cottage-garden plant, grown more for its pungent sweet scent than for its rather insignificant flowers, is supposed to have been introduced to France by Napoleon, who is said to have collected the North African seeds during his Egyptian campaign in order to send them back to the Empress Josephine. Even planted in quite small clumps the small off-white flowers permeate the air and attract the bees with their perfume.

Another shrub well-suited to the white-flowering, evergreen and fragrant theme was *Osmanthus delavayi*, which bears clusters of small, rubular white flowers in April. Planted nearest to the house, they frame the

An ornate *azulejos* fountain set into a stone wall adds a touch of bright colour, the blue of the Portuguese tiles contrasting with the dense green thicket of bamboo and creeper.

front door with their glossy evergreen foliage, toothed like holly leaves. Graceful but slow-growing, they are used here as a substitute for more traditional foundation planting, such as yew or box, and are equally happy in shady conditions.

Clothing the whitewashed façade of the house is a Virginia creeper, tender green in spring and a blaze of scarlet in autumn; and climbing up the side wing to a first-floor terrace are the gnarled, twisting branches of a Chinese wisteria, *W. sinensis* 'Alba'. Mingling with the honeysuckle, it clambers high up a neighbouring stone wall, and produces a spectacular show of fragrant white racemes in April and May.

Above, on the raised terrace by the side of the house swags of Chinese wisteria surround a white-flowering rhododendron.

Opposite, on the right the courtyard's rockery is planted with fragrant creeping alpine plants that grow among the crevices of the volcanic stone.

On the terrace large Italian terracotta pots are grouped to create a secluded garden, overlooking neighbouring gardens and the Panthéon, for a bedroom which gives on to it. Among the light blue lavender and large-leaved viburnums on the terrace are billowing 'Polar Bear' hybrid rhododendrons with clusters of scented pure white flowers.

The owners had to make few structural changes when they decided in 1975 to make this scented garden. The existing curved stone path was extended to the wing and the new entrance hall, and the existing flower beds were considerably reduced in size in order to make a larger cobbled area. To compensate for this loss a great many concrete and terracotta pots and tubs were brought in, and these now contain most of the garden's collection of shrubs. This system has the added advantage of making it possible to provide the specific sun and soil conditions best suited to each plant. Apart from a few plants in very large terracotta troughs, during their flowering periods most are positioned either along the path or in shady corners that need brightening up.

In a sort of enclave off the path, against a corner of the house, is a small circular cobbled area where a round metal table and simple wooden garden chairs add an informal, rustic note. 'Pinxterbloom' azaleas are placed nearby, outside the salon windows, in expectation of their slightly fragrant pink blooms in May. An arching *Forsythia* x *intermedia* 'Spectabilis' to one side of the table blooms after a neighbouring white camellia, and contrasting with them both is a slow-growing evergreen Hinoki cypress, *Chamaecyparis obtusa*, which fills the space with its horizontal branches tipped with rather mannered-looking fan-shaped foliage. In combination with the volcanic lava shapes against which it stands, this Japanese native has a startlingly stylized air. A blood-red *Acer palmatum* 'Sanguineum' nearby adds another surprising note to this otherwise green composition. Its feathery leaves are silhouetted against an evergreen clump of *Pieris japonica* 'Compacta', behind which bloom drifts of late spring-flowering rhododendrons and winter-flowering camellias.

Later in the year small terracotta pots are planted with a collection of scented-leaved pelargoniums, including lemon-scented *P. crispum*, rose-scented *P. capitatum*, and *P.* x *fragrans* with its distinctive ruffled foliage. Placed in empty corners and around the bases of the larger pots, their pink flowers and silvery foliage add to the impression of luxuriant growth and blend perfectly with the garden's white theme. Chosen for its effects of light and airiness in a shady space, this subtle colour scheme seems to shed a pale glow over the garden.

By midsummer the plantings form a shady perfumed tunnel from the street to the house, cooled by refreshing breezes blowing off the fountain and mossy rockery. Neither classical nor cottagy, this modest cobbled courtyard resists simple classification. Highly individual, it is a garden of the imagination, a cool shady spot which seems to capture and hold for a moment fleeting sensations: ephemeral combinations of leaf and flower, and subtle, elusive perfumes.

19

A BAMBOO-FILLED
ORIENTAL GARDEN

VIIe arrondissement

Every year in high summer a stretch of wide boulevard on the *rive gauche* enjoys the deep shade cast by the gnarled, spreading branches and dense foliage of a grove of magnificent *Paulownia tomentosa*. By this time their moment of greatest glory is already over, for the leaves, slender and heart-shaped, unfurl only after the flowers of these exotic, native Chinese trees have faded. In May the fluffy brown buds which the trees bear throughout the winter open to form a dazzling violet-blue canopy of fragrant, foxglove-like flowers, borne in panicles. The effect is breathtaking. No less remarkable is the garden that lies nearby, behind a late nineteenth-century *porte-cochère*. The area in front of the house gives a foretaste of the wealth of unusual planting that lies beyond: a mass of camellias, their ghostly white and shell-pink blooms luminous against their dark leaves, and strands of soaring bamboo transform a rather gloomy courtyard into an exotic jungle. Once over the threshold of the light-filled apartment, the visitor is confronted with a vision of oriental splendour.

Behind the central block of the ground-

Irregularly shaped stepping stones break up the ivy ground cover, while a loquat tree by the salon shades the entrance to the garden.

floor apartment lies a space enclosed on its southern and western sides by the walls of neighbouring gardens, two and a half metres high. On its northern side it is protected by a Virginia creeper-covered wall four storeys high, which shields it from the cold dry

winter winds while allowing the sunlight to flood in from midday onwards.

A decade ago the garden presented a very different picture. Its conventional layout – a patch of lawn surrounded by evergreen and flowering shrubs with the odd group of perennials – was typical of so many town gardens everywhere and took little advantage of the unique qualities of the site.

Its transformation began when the present owner built a long salon wing projecting along the garden's north side, and called in the garden designer Robert Bazelaire. His first move was to blur the edges of the lawn with a rampant ground cover of *Helxine soleirolii*, which quickly formed an undulating blanket of green. Emerging from this, like rocks on the seashore, meandering stepping stones replaced the original straight paths. These weave in and out of an encyclopaedic array of oriental foliage plants, artfully arranged singly and in groups so that the overall effect is one of graceful and natural simplicity. Different leaf forms – large and sculpted or lacily delicate – are juxtaposed in graphic compositions under tall stands of bamboo, which murmur softly in the slightest breeze. Though still evolving, the garden is already completely transformed: a mysteriously veiled light and a powerfully charged atmosphere seem to cling to the elegantly composed plants in this exotic jungle.

This is no slavish imitation of the temple gardens of China or Japan, however, despite the fact that M. Bazelaire has applied similar principles and employed many of the same techniques. Viewed from the salon windows this is a highly personal world, a series of images full of exquisite details and subtle plays on light and shade, depth and perspective. Its vistas are deceptive and its compositions constantly shifting according to the observer's viewpoint; they seem to demand – and to amply repay – quiet contemplation, and their effect is simultaneously soothing and stimulating.

Right, Phyllostachys aureosulcata is just one of more than twenty-five bamboo varieties in the garden.

Previous page left, the jungle-like appearance of the garden is the result of burgeoning growth.

Previous page right, tree ferns shoot in all directions, while the feathery foliage of a Japanese maple adds to the varied growth.

The meandering path traced by the stepping stones is full of small surprises to give visitors a slight jolt and sharpen their perception. Suddenly the solid stone underfoot gives way to a slatted bamboo bridge, or the steady pace is abruptly broken by an unexpectedly large gap between two stones. The visitor's instinctive pause at such points is carefully planned, for invariably there will be close by a half-hidden feature or carefully framed view which demands closer attention.

From one point on the path a plant may seem to be positioned in order to highlight another, and then a few steps further on it will have shifted to reveal a different and unexpected composition. A small *Juniperus horizontalis* 'Bar Harbour', stretching out its long, low, steel-blue branches at ground level, sets off a clump of feathery *Osmunda claytoniana* when seen from one angle, while from another the ferns seem to disappear and the focus is drawn back to the juniper by a stone formation which echoes its low, prostrate shape. This diversity of images and associations created by each plant in relation to the others seems to create an illusory and exaggerated sense both of the size of the garden and of the variety of plants within it. The eye is constantly drawn from one plane to another, from details in the foreground to distant vistas, and from the lianas and bamboos swaying overhead to the froth of helxine and the different materials underfoot.

The overwhelming impression as one enters the garden from the salon is of the profusion of bamboos. No fewer than twenty-five varieties seem to set the garden in perpetual motion, their graceful foliage creating a pale green filigree, trembling and rustling with every breath of wind and filtering the bright sunlight to a milky haze. From the doorway the dense, undulating carpet of *Helxine soleirolii* spreads outwards to engulf most of the garden, surrounding stepping stones and bonsai trees in pots, and

creating a vivid emerald-green backcloth for the rest of the planting.

A tall loquat tree, *Eriobotrya japonica*, a Chinese native pruned to its present shape over many years, frames the French windows. From its branches hang baskets

of trailing staghorn fern, *Platycerium bifurcatum* and *Sedum morganianum*, and above it there rises a great cloud of clipped honeysuckle. A *Jasminum* x *stephanese*, which bears sweetly scented pink flowers in June, twists up the wall of the salon wing, among the thick, woody stems and graceful foliage of the wisteria and the spear-shaped leaves of *Hedera helix* 'Mandel's Crested'.

The garden has two main areas: a shady part near the house and a circular open lawn at the bottom. Defining the junction between the two are a pair of trees which formed part of the garden's original planting: a tall horse chestnut, heavily pruned to an almost columnar form, and in front of it

A spreading weeping willow shades the centre of the garden while a dense bank of rhododendrons and camellias screens the far reaches from the house.

At the garden's far corner the entrance to the teahouse is marked by a bamboo bridge and a Japanese water basin.

an arching white willow, *Salix alba* 'Tristis', which casts a dappled shade on the two-metre-square pool beneath. Between them, thriving in the half-shade, are mounds of pale pink- and white-flowering rhododendrons, with their lower growth thinned, or 'carved' as M. Bazelaire terms the technique, to expose the striking patterns formed by their dark branches. In front of the rhododendrons, and in full view of the entrance, is a swathe of camellias in shades of pink,

which, with their dense, dark foliage, create an almost solid backdrop for the aquatic grasses and ferns planted in and around the pool. White water lilies float on the surface, among tufts of umbrella grass, *Cyperus alternifolius*, surrounded by small clumps of variegated Japanese sedge, *Carex morrowii* 'Aureo-variegata', and Japanese sweet flax, *Acorus gramineus* 'Variegatus', rising from the rolling mounds of helxine. By mid-March, when the fronds of the large collection of ferns are beginning to unfurl, the emerald green carpet is dotted with yellow, blue and white primulas and the pale blue and white bracts of *Hyacinthus amethystinus* and *H. a.* 'Albus', which seed freely on the moist banks of the pool.

In a shady corner, tight up against the apartment wall, and beyond a *Pieris formosa* 'Forestii' clipped into a ball-shape and underplanted with hostas, is a secluded spot which has been transformed into a thicket of bamboo. Among the dark green culms are a pure black *Phyllostachys nigra* and a contrasting pale yellow *P. viridis* 'Robert Young'. Some of the black bamboo stems have been cut half way up to produce low tufts of leaves which seem to float above the helxine ground cover. Throughout the year a group of highly polished grey and brown-streaked pebbles rise from the creeper like rocks on a beach at low tide, and in spring pale pink impatiens with rose-pink centres are bedded out randomly, to form pillows of softly glowing colour by summer. This composition on several levels makes a carefully balanced frame for views of the garden, with the light-filled open lawn in the distance, while the receding planes of different shades of green make a soothing prospect from the apartment's windows.

Running the length of the garden's southern perimeter is a bank of bamboo, making a graphic forest of verticals of different heights and colours. At their foot a winding stream, made by M. Bazelaire five years ago, is planted here and there with drifts of variegated dwarf bamboo, sheared in winter to promote dense growth in spring. Outcrops of Japanese maples, *Acer palmatum* 'Dissectum Ornatum' and *A.p.* 'Lanciniatum', osmundas and nandina, the Chinese sacred bamboo, add a light, feathery texture to the bamboos, which include *Phyllostachys pubescens* 'Heterocycla' and *P. aureosulcata*, with its extraordinary crooked stems. Three *Betula albo-sinensis* rise towards the back of the bank, against a bamboo screen erected to

mask the stone walls. With their pale trunks glowing with light orange and pink reflections, the unusual Chinese paper birch give an illusion of added depth and height to the bamboo grove. Here tufts of white impatiens spread to form softly luminous mounds at ground level, reflecting the filtered sunlight that penetrates this cool area in summer.

The stream flows past groups of rocks set into the helxine and planted with angular

evergreen conifers such as the blue Colorado spruce, *Picea pungens* 'Glauca', and dwarf Hinoki cypress, *Chamaecyparis obtusa* 'Nana Variegata'. Looming over the tall bamboos are the remains of an old tree, which in late March becomes a mass of pale pink, as the *Clematis montana* 'Rubens' that has climbed up it over the years bursts into flower, shrouding the gnarled branches and hanging down into the bamboo below.

In a far corner a slatted bamboo bridge

A shady corner of this oriental garden is marked by the striking yellow culms of bamboo that frame the view. Underfoot, the ground cover is a profuse mixture of stepping stones, pebbles and ivy.

leads over the narrow stream to a teahouse, which affords sheltered views of the garden, framed by two large red Japanese maples, *Acer palmatum* 'Dissectum atropurpureum'. A bamboo *tsukubai* or Japanese water basin catches a trickle of water that flows from a tall bamboo pole, its splashing echoing the gurgling of the stream.

In the corner opposite the teahouse and in direct view of the entrance, a weeping birch, *Betula pendula* 'Tristis', rises above a group of Japanese maples, pruned to allow views deep into the shady corner bed. Another weeping birch, *B. p.* 'Gracilis', with deeply cut leaves, frames the view on the other side, while a third birch, *B. albo-sinensis* rises in the far corner. In spring the visitor's first view on entering the garden is of brilliant white azaleas, etched against the green and translucent red maple and birch foliage, which then gives way to a softer vision of delicate pink camellias. This small area sets the tone, both literally and figuratively, for the rest of the garden, for it encapsulates the range of tones and play of contrasting foliage forms on which M. Bazelaire has based the design.

Along the Virginia creeper-covered north wall a loquat tree shades a corkscrew hazel, *Corylus avellana* 'Contorta', set against the spiralling evergreen foliage of a dwarf Hinoki

cypress. Dramatic tree ferns and stands of various bamboo arch over the lawn area, the latter including green-and-yellow striped *Phyllostachys viridis* 'Robert Young' and a large clump of the green and golden-brown tortoiseshell-patterned *P. nigra* 'Boryana'. The graceful foliage mingles with the shoots of a black bamboo and tendrils of clematis to form a cascading canopy over a garden bench and Chinese ceramic stools arranged below.

Wherever one looks in this garden there are imaginative associations of unusual plants, from the broad-leaved hostas growing against the feathery evergreen mounds of Sawara cypress, *Chamaecyparis pisifera* 'Plumosa', to the bonsai crab apples in a landscape of boulders and spreading helxine. A deceptive sense of lush, uncontrolled growth and spontaneous change reigns, for this living scene from an oriental painting was carefully planned by M. Bazelaire, and retains the seemingly careless air only by means of constant maintenance and control. A place for peaceful walks and for attentive observation, for relaxation and for concentration, this is a garden of paradoxes, a natural-seeming artefact designed as much for stimulation as for contemplation.

A simple garden bench, flanked by bright blue and white chinese porcelain stools provides a quiet spot among the tangled vines and bamboo foliage.

Below left, a pendulous birch, pruned annually by M. Bazelaire, floats above the airy branches of the Japanese maples and mounds of dwarf bamboo.

Right, the pond full of water lilies is framed by water grasses and arched fern fronds.

20

A GARDEN OF THEATRICAL SURPRISES

M. Roger Chapelain-Midy
V^e arrondissement

Over the past fifty years and more, Roger Chapelain-Midy, the celebrated artist and theatrical designer, has created in the garden of his Parisian retreat a world of the imagination, of fantasy and of innovation, full of theatrical surprises and distinctive touches of whimsy. Viewed from M. Chapelain-Midy's attic studio, at the far end of the early nineteenth-century house, it stands as testimony to his painterly eye and his theatrical instincts, as well as to his great passion for gardens.

'I was completely overwhelmed when I walked in off the street, and saw a pear tree covered in pale pink blossom', says Chapelain-Midy of the spring day in 1934 when he first discovered the secluded garden. Set back from the Rue Lhomond, the three-storey house and its garden plot are protected on all sides by the white-painted façades of neighbouring buildings, which shield them from the noises of the city. The sloping site, on the steep southern edge of the *V^e arrondissement*, is tightly wedged between other houses with an equally rural air, lying concealed behind the street frontage.

The long, narrow granite path from the garden gate is bordered by beds edged with ivy and ends under an arch of cherry laurel, *Prunus laurocerasus*, and ivy, which makes a dramatic frame for the pink-painted house beyond. The glossy evergreen leaves of the laurel make a particularly fine screen, which in spring is covered with small white flowers in long racemes.

The colour scheme in the narrow bed that borders the path changes throughout the year. In mid-March it is pure white with drifts of *Narcissus* x *incomparabilis*, which are followed by tulips massed in contrasting blocks of bright colours. Mendel tulips, including the red-orange 'Bestseller' and deep carmine 'Pink Trophy', flower in late April and early May, mingled with late-flowering yellow *Hyacinthus orientalis* 'City of Haarlem'. Later in the year roses bloom recurrently throughout the summer, with the pink-tinged Hybrid perpetual 'Oskar Cordel' and the coral-rose Grandiflora 'Enchanted Autumn' creating variations on a pink theme.

Beyond the laurel arch a rectangular granite-paved terrace opens out, arranged with delicate white-painted wrought-iron furniture. Leading off it, narrow paths edged in box disappear into the dense surrounding shrubbery. Dividing the rectangular garden into two distinct areas, Chapelain-Midy has planted clumps of variegated Japanese aucuba, *A. japonica* 'Variegata', which have grown to great heights over the years. These common shrubs are here treated in an unorthodox manner, creating a novel effect while at the same time adding a dimension of height to the space. Pruned annually to encourage growth, their sturdy branches make dramatic dark silhouettes, bearing tufts or yellow-speckled evergreen foliage. Laurels, all too often seen as a densely compact utilitarian shrub, good for using where nothing else will grow, here are transformed into light, airy plants, their scarlet berries providing colour at eye level in win-

Above, from the ivy-covered archway the garden opens up to reveal a number of whimsical features.

Opposite, viewed from the street entrance the house lies half hidden behind dense foliage.

Previous page left, a colourful bed of tulips, hyacinths and narcissi runs the length of the granite path.

Previous page right, detail of the ornate, the nineteenth-century white wrought iron bench which adds another splash of colour to the garden.

Apart from the irresistible pear tree, the large space, twenty metres by thirty metres, was utterly devoid of vegetation, a state of affairs which M. Chapelain-Midy has taken great care to remedy over the years. Applying the same principles that he has used throughout his distinguished career as a set designer, and adapting them with his customary artistic flair, he designed a layout for the garden. In it he incorporated a number of theatrical devices, including tricks of perspective and scale, proportion and colour, which give it an unpredictable, constantly surprising air.

A dark green trellised fence and a solid black iron gate, flanked by square stone pillars supporting decorative urns, run the length of the small courtyard, screening the garden from the street. The trellis is densely planted with ivy and laurel, protecting the garden's privacy, while at the same time allowing glimpses of the delights within.

Surrounded by the deep shade of a Japanese fatsia and viburnums a fruit-bearing statue suddenly emerges, another of the garden's whimsical elements.

ter. Underplanted with spring-flowering bulbs and *Bergenia purpurascens*, with pink flowers in April and May and bold glossy foliage that turns deep red in autumn and winter, the laurels form a tall screen around the semicircular lawn between the house and courtyard.

Behind the lawn, hidden in an arbour of many shades of green, a terracotta statue suddenly appears, a distant focal point. Framed by the contrasting foliage of a spreading *Viburnum davidii*, with long, oval dark green leaves and a *Fatsia japonica*, with light green leaves, the small female figure creates a distorted sense of perspective,

highlighted when she is viewed from the entrance path. She stands in a densely planted grove of evergreens, chosen for their disparate leaf shapes and contrasting tones of green, which together produce a display of lush exuberance. As with his use of laurels, M. Chapelain-Midy here uses humble 'useful' plants, which are very often the last resort of the town gardener battling with poor light and soil, and with them creates exciting and even extravagant effects. With his eye for composition and form, he has a talent for the unexpected and the unconventional. Through his skilful use of the illusory qualities of tricks of light and shade, he makes the garden's evergreen framework come alive. The plants that frame the statue – from the towering blue-tinged Lawson cypress, the flowering ornamental cherry and the viburnum to the bank of bergenia, *Syringa vulgaris* 'Souvenir de Louis Späth' and fatsia opposite – are staggered in height, so leading the eye to the focal point. Backlit, their varied colours and forms clearly differentiated, they stand sharply silhouetted against each other.

Another feature which uses the powerful effects of light and shade to create an air of mystery is the stone well that stands next to the Lawson cypress. American elder, *Sambucus canadensis*, trained over the circular well-head, with years of pruning has formed an umbrella-shaped canopy which casts deep shadows under the feature. The intriguing mound of dark green foliage, sprinkled in autumn with purple-black berries, screens a small greenhouse and the compost heap.

In spring clumps of iris, imported specially from England, flower vivid blue and yellow in serpentine beds encircling the greenhouse and the cypress, and bordering the semicircular lawn.

A narrow earth path, edged with a low metal fence to protect the precious grass against the household dog, winds through the jungle of contrasting foliage to return to the granite terrace. Beside this, in the middle of a rectangular lawn under the main garden façade of the house, a female figure emerges from a mound of glossy-leaved Persian ivy, *Hedera colchica*. Clipped to her waist like a voluminous green crinoline, the ivy billows down to a circular pool beneath her. The leafily-clad naiad, seemingly floating on the water's shimmering surface, is another enigmatic player in the mysterious drama that suffuses this garden. A dark, curving yew hedge provides a suitable backdrop.

Horse chestnut trees, severely pruned and standing against the neighbouring stone wall, cast dappled shadows on the figure and her grassy stage. Against this wall, at the

In the centre of the lawn, surrounded by lush, shady foliage, a female figure emerges from a mound of Persian ivy. Beyond stands the aviary, a traditional garden feature since classical times.

The bed along the edge of the carefully tended lawn adds yet more colour to this vivid garden.

garden's far end and under the canopy of the chestnut trees, M. Chapelain-Midy has built a large aviary, which he filled with a collection of small birds.

Aviaries have been a traditional garden feature since classical times, and by the sixteenth cenury they were popular in Italy and at the courts of Europe. A century later, at Versailles, a pair of two-storey aviaries with ornate gilt ironwork and tented roofs were constructed for Louis XIV in the *cour de marbre* and stocked with exotic singing birds. Following the zoological and botanical expeditions of the nineteenth century many large-scale aviaries were built in public parks

Left, detail of the terracotta statue that is set against the simply patterned façade of the small pavilion.

across Europe. Elaborately conceived and constructed, many of them sought to re-create the birds' natural environment, as at the Jardin des Plantes in Paris.

M. Chapelain-Midy's aviary, like the nineteenth-century pavilions at the Jardin des Plantes, has an air of enchantment, which the fantastic grotto-like construction it contains does nothing to dispel. Against the back wall, which he has painted sky blue, the painter has built a petrified lava flow. From a fountain at the top, a stream of water cascades over its crevices and crags, filling the shady corner with its splashing and murmuring.

Behind the curved yew hedge, in the far corner of the garden, rises a small half-timbered pavilion, rather like the make-believe cottages in Marie Antoinette's 'vil-lage' at Versailles, Le Petit Hameau, and with the same dreamlike atmosphere. Half-hidden among the chestnut trees and dis-creetly shrouded by a grape vine, it exerts a subtly romantic influence on this corner of the garden.

Concerns about maintenance and poor growing conditions dictated M. Chapelain-

Midy's choice of hardy evergreen shrubs as the framework for his garden. While the two lawns require a certain amount of upkeep, the laurels, viburnums, fatsia and rhododen-drons planted near the ivy-covered arch need little attention. Bedding plants among the mounds of evergreen shrubbery, includ-ing sweet williams, impatiens and asters, add colour to the garden; and terracotta lions, cast-iron urns, and brilliant white-painted garden seats and bird cages, provide ex-tremely decorative effects and intricate sil-houettes against curtains and swags of som-bre foliage.

Amid M. Chapelain-Midy's leafy set pieces, the garden seems miraculously trans-formed at every turn of the path, and with each new vista. This series of inter-connecting 'rooms', each separate and hid-den, and yet all sharing a secret symbolism, transcends any normal definition of a gar-den. A place of elusive atmospheres and surreal tableaux, of perceptual tricks and metaphysical games, it seems to break the bonds of the urban landscape that surround it, and to escape into a world of the imagination.

Opposite, a white wrought iron bird cage adds to the garden's air of fantasy.

21

A RAMBLING
COUNTRY GARDEN

Mme Philippe Dauchez
V^e arrondissement

Down the southern slopes of the Montagne Sainte-Geneviève, below the Panthéon and just above the Latin Quarter in the *V^e arrondissement*, meanders the Rue Mouffetard. It follows the course of a Roman road, part of the network that linked Lutece, as the Romans called Paris, to Lyon and on to Italy. Gradually, the original fortified settlement situated on the Île de la Cité expanded on to both banks of the river Seine. By the ninth century, the southern slopes of the Montagne Sainte-Geneviève were cultivated with vineyards, most of which during the

course of the following centuries came under the control of the powerful religious orders which became established there, linked to the city by the main thoroughfare of the Rue Mouffetard. The narrow cobbled lanes that wind down the hill retain their medieval street plan and a special character unique in Paris.

'There was never any reason for us to leave for the country in August like so many Parisians. We always stayed here, where it was like the country itself', recalls Mme Dauchez of the garden she and her late

husband, the painter and naval architect Philippe Dauchez, created together. The perfect complement to the rural atmosphere of the area, it could easily be a country garden tucked away in some small hamlet in the depths of the countryside.

The horizons of this intrepid couple have always stretched far beyond the French countryside, however. They shared a passion for the sea and everything to do with it: dedicated sailors, they collected on their many voyages (including three crossings of the Atlantic with just one extra crew member) an assortment of shells and other mementoes, which crowd their ground-floor apartment. And the sea was also Philippe Dauchez's chief inspiration as a painter; after every voyage he returned home to paint, and to find peace in the garden retreat that he and his wife created over a period of thirty years.

The Dauchez's building is set back from the street and its noise behind the *porte-cochère* of a mid-nineteenth-century mansion

The entrance to the secluded garden is marked by an ivy-covered portal which immediately instils a cottage-garden atmosphere that pervades the entire plot.

Previous page left, the studio into which Philippe Dauchez would retreat to paint after his sea voyages lies concealed in a far corner of the garden, covered in lush ivy and purple-flowering campanulas.

Previous page right, potted plants are surrounded by a sea of ivy.

Below, the dense plantings of purple-flowering campanulas, spreading ferns and clumps of iris, as well as delicate pinkish-peach rose blossoms create a rural atmosphere around the studio.

block on the Rue Mouffetard. Fenced off to the right of the paved inner courtyard is a small vegetable and flower garden, the private domain of the *concierge*. The tiny garden, bursting with scarlet roses and giant yellow sunflowers, tall Brussel sprouts and feathery carrot tops, recalls the modest 'allotments' to be seen on railway embankments in the Parisian suburbs. Each rectangular plot is a masterpiece of meticulous organization, divided into pocket-sized compartments, each crammed with a different fruit or vegetable; each is carefully tended and lovingly maintained, and sometimes is clearly valued as much as a means of personal expression as for its usefulness.

Beyond the courtyard is the Dauchez's apartment, from which their land rises steeply up the slopes of the Montagne Sainte-Geneviève. Although generous in size for a town garden, at six hundred metres, the rectangular site presented a number of difficulties. After climbing up the sharp incline the land flattens out at the far end, making a

high plateau looking down over the apartment. A concrete retaining wall, built to support the bank, runs the width of the garden, facing the French windows which punctuate the house façade. A low privet hedge, planted to camouflage the wall, marks the junction between the terrace and the bank. After lengthy deliberations the Dauchezs decided to grass the slope, with the result that the French windows frame a tableau of green throughout the year. Most of the planting has been restricted to either end, in order to keep the wide, park-like expanse clear and uncluttered. Early-flowering shrubs such as forsythia and *Magnolia stellata*, planted halfway down the bank, announce the arrival of spring. The forsythia's mass of golden flowers and the magnolia's star-shaped fragrant blooms, both borne on bare branches, are set off to full advantage against the simple green background.

To the left of the terrace, a wide and imposing flight of shallow, mossy stone steps rises to the higher level. It is mirrored at the opposite end of the terrace by some narrow, rustic steps with a rickety wooden handrail, which zigzags slightly drunkenly up the steep slope. At the top the two flights of steps are joined by an earth path which crosses the plateau and runs right round the garden. On the level plateau it meanders around circular and oval beds planted with spring bulbs and summer-flowering perennials. Clumps of violet-blue and purple crocuses and masses of pale yellow narcissi are followed in May and June by rose-pink *Lilium rubellum*, pale pink peonies and pink floribunda roses.

For a while the path follows a stone party-wall festooned with ivy and punctuated at intervals with pale green mounds of laurel, interspersed with scarlet-flowering camellias. The camellias' waxy dark green foliage forms a contrast with the laurels' larger, paler leaves, and their blooms are brilliant spots of colour against the green background. More colour is provided in

The serpentine path that winds along the garden's highest level is planted in spring with bright red and yellow tulips. Bergenias also burst forth with purple-pink blossoms while the variegated aucubas provide contrasting greenery.

fera, planted over thirty years ago as tiny seedlings, and one of M. Dauchez's earliest efforts in the garden. The tall, graceful trees add interest to the far corner of the garden, especially in winter, when their ghostly white trunks glimmer softly in the pale sunlight.

At the northern end of the garden the path curves past the entrance to M. Dauchez's secret garden, containing his studio. A two-and-a-half-metre-high arch covered with ivy screens it from the rest of the garden, and in turn is shaded by evergreen holly trees and a spreading False Acacia, *Robina pseudo-acacia*, which cloak this secluded area in mystery. Low terraced beds rise to the floor of the glass-panelled studio, which rests against the stone wall of a neighbouring building. *Campanula* billows softly in the shady beds, and cascades over the terraces, its tiny purple-pink flowers creating a subtle haze of colour in May. In spring red and yellow primulas and yellow daffodils poke through the ground cover, followed by clusters of pale purple sweet williams. Blue flag irises, sword ferns, wild hyacinths and dashing single red tulips are also dotted about, seemingly at random, to create a luminous *pointilliste* effect. The studio itself hides romantically behind a bed of roses, while ivy and a grapevine scrabble over the pitched corrugated iron roof. An Austrian pine, *Pinus nigra*, and an untrained yew add their deep green camouflage to the garden's defences, shielding it from view throughout the year.

spring by the vivid yellow and red tulips and yellow and white daffodils that border the path. Planted at irregular intervals, they provide staccato bursts of luminous colour, brightening the view from the apartment windows after the long dark days of winter. In the warmer days that follow, spring flowers give way to begonias in sizzling shades of red and pink. 'We wanted colour in the garden, and not one of those lifeless monochromatic schemes that are so fashionable these days', remarks Mme Dauchez. There is nothing rare or temperamental about the plants in her garden: these are common-or-garden varieties, chosen and used for their unrivalled ability to bring dark and distant corners alive with loud splashes of colour.

On the other side of the path, opposite the camellias and the flowerbeds is a group of three towering paper birch, *Betula papyri-*

The striking effects of strong colour and varied leaf shape are the result of the Dauchez's clear vision and careful planning. They did all the work themselves, but now Mme Dauchez relies on her friend Jacques Valdi to help her. Together they sit down in early winter to plan new plantings and work for the coming season, concentrating over the past few years on thinning out overgrown shrubs and pruning trees to allow more light to penetrate the garden.

The garden has an informal feel to it, and an air of discovery and surprise. It encourages leisurely walks and gentle rambles, the path forever leading on to startling combinations of colour and shape, and tempting the visitor into hidden corners, seemingly far away from the surrounding city. All too close and still encroaching – there is a new building just outside the garden walls – the urban landscape still cannot impinge on the atmosphere of this *rus in urbe*, this little patch of countryside in the city. In this garden, so personal in conception and apparently simple in execution, M. and Mme Dauchez created a haven from the buffetings both of Atlantic storms and of city life.

Flanking one end of the apartment's terrace a wide flight of steps rises to the garden's upper levels.

22

A FORMAL SEVENTEENTH-CENTURY GARDEN

Baron and Baroness Guy de Rothschild
IVᵉ arrondissement

The Baron and Baroness Guy de Rothschild's Paris home, Hôtel Lambert, standing at the eastern end of the Île Saint-Louis, is among the most perfectly appointed seventeenth-century private homes in the city. Since they bought the *hôtel* in 1976, the Rothschilds have undertaken a comprehensive scheme of restoration, embracing the building itself (officially classified as a *monument historique*), its interior decoration and the garden, taking care in every aspect of the work to remain faithful to the classical principles that inspired this

remarkable ensemble. As a result the Hôtel Lambert now stands restored to a condition which must surely approach its original splendour.

Begun in 1642, the building and its grounds have direct links with Louis XIV, for they were conceived and designed by many of the same artists and craftsmen who built Versailles a mere twenty years later. The ambitious young king cannot have been unaware of the work in progress at the Hôtel Lambert as he started planning his monumental château.

Opposite, creating a sense of greater depth, a row of cone-shaped yews flanks the shaded path that leads round the garden, while black-painted iron benches are placed formally between the row of horse chestnut trees.

Previous page left, the cone- and pyramid-shaped yews encircle the garden's central feature – a low, stone rimmed fountain and *miroir d'eau*.

Previous page right, under the dappled shade of lime trees and hidden from the *hôtel particulier* by rows of yew, a secluded seating area lies near the garden's river side.

Over the centuries, this house has not only been associated with some of the most remarkable architects and designers in French history, but also with a number of distinguished occupants, including Voltaire and Jean-Jacques Rousseau (not to mention a manufacturer of mattresses and a girls' orphanage).

In 1642 a flamboyant financier, Jean-Baptiste Lambert, hired a thirty-year-old up-and-coming architect, Louis Le Vau, to build a grand *hôtel particulier* on an irregular site on the newly developed Île Saint-Louis. Two years later he died, and the land and building works were inherited by his brother, Nicolas Lambert, President of the French Supreme Court in charge of public expenditure.

It was Nicolas Lambert who was responsible for bringing together the extraordinarily talented team of young men who between them created some of France's greatest achievements in the fields of architecture and landscape design. Lambert hired Le Vau's friends and contemporaries to complete his *hôtel*: he engaged the twenty-three-year-old Charles Lebrun to paint a ceiling depicting the labours of Hercules; Eustache Le Sueur, then twenty-two, to paint panels, ornaments and grotesques on the walls of the Cabinet de l'Amour and the Cabinet des Muses; and the Dutch decorative sculptor Von Obstel to design the stucco work.

This youthful team also collaborated on work at the Louvre, the Tuileries and Vaux-le-Vicomte, the massive château and formal gardens – the first of the great formal gardens – which were to prove the downfall of Nicolas Fouquet, Louis XIV's superintendent of finance. In 1666 Fouquet gave a *fête* for the king at his new château, at which the royal retinue was entertained and dazzled by waterworks, fireworks, music by Lully, a new play by Molière, and above all by the sheer splendour of the setting. It was the last such evening either the château or its

owner was to see, for at a time in his reign when he was beginning to display the despotic side to his character, Louis was as much piqued and enraged by his subject's hubris as he was impressed by his achievement. Two weeks later Fouquet was arrested and imprisoned on charges of embezzlement, and his close associate Nicolas Lambert was fined for related offences.

André Le Nôtre, the inspired designer responsible for the gardens at Vaux, is not linked to the gardens at the Hôtel Lambert by any documentary evidence. But the circumstantial evidence is persuasive: just as Lambert and Fouquet were associates, so Lebrun was close friends with Le Nôtre, then twenty-nine years old. It is not impossible that Le Vau, Lebrun and Le Nôtre collaborated on the Lambert project just as they did on their more grandiose royal commissions. With or without Le Nôtre, the Hôtel Lambert's designers certainly worked together as partners and as Pierre Nolhac, chief curator of Versailles at the beginning of the century, wrote, 'They shared a fraternal genius.' It is clear that the theories which underlie the compositions of Vaux-le-Vicomte and Versailles are also those which were applied to the smaller but equally noble Hôtel Lambert. Its dramatic grandeur is the result of a philosophy of architecture which attempts to synthesize interior and exterior design elements, in which indoor and outdoor spaces are of equal importance and complementary value to the overall concept.

Faced with the obvious problems of a sloping, irregular-shaped site on the river embankment, Le Vau set out to turn these disadvantages to his advantage. He conceived the notion of a private residence filled with architectural surprises in which both the river and garden played major roles. He also distinguished Hôtel Lambert from its neighbours by a clever reversal of structural thinking. As he was responsible for the design not only of the nearby church of Saint-Louis, but also for the Hôtel Hesselin,

the Hôtel Lauzun and a number of modest buildings (including his own home), Le Vau devised a plan in which he sited all the structures alongside the river with their gardens behind them, with one sole exception. The Hôtel Lambert's river-front garden was revolutionary: the core of the building is set back from the water by some seventy-five metres, in a position which clearly sets it apart – both literally and figuratively – from its neighbours, while at the same time emphasizing its stately scale.

The forbidding street façade is punctuated with a two-storey *porte à voussure*, or arched carriage entrance, and decorated with grotesque masks, lions' heads and palm leaves,

signifying victory. Inside, a courtyard curves round an imposing central pavilion, which accentuates the *hôtel*'s symmetrically placed principal axis. A short flight of steps leads to a landing, from which a majestic double staircase rises to the first of the *hôtel*'s principal floors. To reach the *piano nobile*, the visitor has to pass through a vast domed pavilion, where Le Vau played brilliantly with the dramatic juxtapositioning of different volumes of light and dark.

A second-floor landing overlooking the courtyard leads to an oval antechamber; this in turn opens on the Galerie d'Hercule, thirty-five metres long and flanked with floor-to-ceiling windows, which terminates

The principles that governed seventeenth-century French garden design were applied rigorously by the Baron and Baroness Rothschild when they restored the Hôtel Lambert. Based on order and symmetry, the garden layout mirrors the architectural style of the *hôtel*'s façades.

in a huge bow window framing a panorama of the river. Rippling reflections dance on the gilded walls and painted ceiling, softening to a limpid glow towards evening. The gallery seems to float high above the Seine and the garden below, which, peaceful and orderly, is a constant reaffirmation of the classical principles which govern the ensemble. Over the centuries this spectacular gallery has been the setting for some of Europe's most celebrated dinners and balls.

From the second floor, the garden is seen in perfect perspective, an artfully enclosed space regulated by pure lines and geometric shapes. When the French architectural critic Pierre Lavendan wrote, 'a garden *à la française* is a lesson in order', he might very well have been inspired by this vision. Raised about five metres to the level of the *hôtel*'s first principal floor, the garden terrace is thus dissociated from life at street level: visually, physically and psychologically, it is on a higher plane. In the seventeenth century, when viewed from the *hôtel*, the river views formed a logical and visual continuum with the garden, at once contrasting with its sober greens and increasing its scale. In order to set the scene for a noble perspective, and at the same time to ensure privacy, Le Vau erected a screen along the length of the garden's street side, creating a sort of mirror image of the Galerie d'Hercule wing.

When Marie-Hélène and Guy de Rothschild bought the *hôtel* in 1976 the river views had changed considerably from the panorama which had formed part of Le Vau's scheme. The Port de Sully, built during the nineteenth century, now bisects the island at its easternmost point, passing underneath the Hôtel Lambert's garden. The bucolic pastoral river landscape has disappeared under bricks and mortar; the Rothschilds therefore wanted to screen the immediate view without losing the special light and sense of buoyancy that the river creates.

The garden, too, had undergone a number of distressing changes since Le Vau's time.

At one point a disturbing glass-and-iron spiral staircase was clamped on to the façade, linking the first and second floors; and a nineteenth-century resident had planted a mulberry tree next to the central fountain. When the Rothschilds arrived it had grown to such a size that it completely obscured the entire central area of the garden, so they had it removed.

Gradually, they simplified the garden greatly, together with the garden façades, where they restored Le Vau's original Ionic pilasters, designed to be viewed from across the river on the right bank. Despite thorough searching, the Rothschilds were unable to find any of Le Vau's drawings to guide them in re-creating the garden, so they consulted instead the plans of the Hôtel Lambert published in François Blondel's 1752 treatise, *Architecture Française*.

Many seventeenth-century garden techniques are used to recapture the spirit of the

Ivy climbs the tree trunks from the bed below but is clipped deliberately to the height of the ivy-covered wall behind, reinforcing both the garden's formal style and its all-green scheme.

Hôtel Lambert's classical design. The existing chestnut and lime trees are pleached in early spring to control their growth and create architectural shapes, a method still practised widely throughout France in public parks and on tree-lined streets. Thus trained, the trees here provide maximum protection from the urban views without closing the garden in. The lower branches of trees along the garden's river side are pruned to a height of two and a half metres from the ground, and their crowns are clipped to a rectangular shape. The ivy which twines up the trunks is trimmed at the height of the lowest branches, so that when seen from the ground-floor salons the geometric green shapes seem to be supported on equally spaced green trunks. More ivy, planted to camouflage two-metre railings which run along the garden's river and street sides, has been clipped over the years to form a dense, even curtain.

The focal point of the garden's central space is a shallow round pool with a small, urn-shaped stone fountain. Traditionally known as a *miroir d'eau*, the pool reflects the sky and surrounding greenery, and is framed by a wide granite lip. Four small jets break the surface of the water, their gentle trickling emphasizing the quiet of the garden and echoing the river beyond.

The pool is set in a smooth grass square, bisected at right angles by two paths of crushed off-white gravel, which meet another path encircling the pool. The four grass areas, edged with granite blocks, form a sharply defined, rigidly symmetrical pattern, punctuated at intervals by flawless pyramids and cones of yew.

Topiary, a technique that goes back to ancient Greece, was one of the seventeenth-century garden designer's battery of tools for the control of man over nature. For what more complete expression of man's mastery could there be than the shaping of nature's riotous forms into severely geometric lines and planes, arranged in relentlessly rational patterns? The garden here has become part of the overall architecture, its manicured shapes and their plays of light and shade heightening its drama; its cool symmetry echoing the classical balance of the whole.

The two-metre-high yew pyramids at the Hôtel Lambert stand like sentinels at three-metre intervals around the perimeter of the grass area, seemingly guarding the inner space while framing views of the fountain. In the centre of each bed is a cone-shaped yew, three and a half metres high, creating a play of heights and volumes, light and shade. The yews, ivy and grass are green throughout the year, and the shapes retain their mass and volume, so crucial to the *hôtel*'s setting.

There is no other colour in this garden. The varying tones of green, in accordance with the strict principles practised by Le Nôtre, create a scene of perfect balance and harmony, reflecting and enhancing the architecture of the *hôtel* itself. The garden of the Hôtel Lambert has been turned once more into a restrained and harmonious backdrop to one of the finest expressions of French classical architecture.

Right, framed by meticulously clipped evergreens an Antique bust stands in the distance against a backdrop of ivy. Behind, the wall that encloses the garden mirrors the architectural style of the wing of the house opposite. The vase-shaped fountain with four masked spouts resembles the large stone urns that once stood along the roof edge of the Hôtel Lambert.

The long Galerie d'Hercule on the *hôtel*'s first floor offers panoramic views of Paris, yet behind the carefully clipped hedges the garden lies undisturbed by the bustle of the city.

23

AN ALL-WHITE GARDEN

Mme Hélène Rochas
VIIe arrondissement

Set against a broad horizon of green foliage and the open sky, broken only by a glimpse of the gilt dome of the Hôtel des Invalides, Hélène Rochas's all-white garden in the Faubourg Saint-Germain is a superb example of a formal Parisian garden. The garden's special atmosphere, serene and elegant, is largely achieved by its white theme, which remains pure and constant as the seasons change and one flower succeeds another. Azaleas and rhododendrons, roses and tulips, chrysanthemums and wisteria, camellias and clematis, all are white: 'My

favourite flowers for the house have always been white. That was what made me decide to have the garden done in completely one colour.'

One-colour gardens have a prominent place in the history of twentieth-century garden design. Mme Rochas's inspiration came from two of the most celebrated, both across the Channel: Hidcote and Sissinghurst. Both include axial walks leading to a series of geometrically shaped 'rooms' enclosed by clipped hedges, usually of beech, hornbeam, or yew, and containing a variety of planting schemes, each arranged in subtle combinations of colour and foliage. Many of the elements of the famous 'White Garden' at Sissinghurst, with its box-edged, geometrically shaped beds planted with white-flowering iris, peonies, tobacco plants, lilies and roses with clumps of silver-grey and green foliage, may be seen here, on a much reduced scale.

A two-metre-high stone wall, clothed with flowering climbers and curtains of ivy, separates the series of small enclosures from what was once part of the vast gardens of the neighbouring eighteenth-century Hôtel de Biron, now the Rodin Museum. Built on open marshland by Jean Aubert and Jacques Gabriel, this majestic *hôtel particulier* radically transformed the Faubourg Saint-Germain into an area of elegant *hôtels* set in noble surroundings. The Hôtel de Biron's gardens had formal parterres opening on to a large lake with serpentine paths leading to a wooded area to create a *jardin à l'anglaise*. Neglected during the nineteenth century and restored in 1924, they stand as a magnificent reminder of the gardens that used to be typical of the area, lying hidden behind the classical street façades. They also make an exceptional backdrop for Mme Rochas's garden, even providing a tall expanse of white-flowering horse chestnuts.

'Even from inside, all you can see are the tree tops of the Hôtel de Biron and sky', says Mme Rochas of the extraordinary views that fill her salon windows. The low, tree-filled horizon completely obscures the surrounding city, creating a potent illusion of space and isolation. Flooded with the filtered light which seems to be unique to Paris, and filled with all-white flowers, this garden seems to be a place apart, with its own intoxicating atmosphere.

The layout dates to 1970, when Mme Rochas built a small annexe at one end of the rectangular space. 'Before then, the garden resembled a miniature public park, crisscrossed with curved gravel paths and loud municipal-style plantings, which seemed to reduce it in size and disrupted the views from the interior. What I wanted was a light, airy effect which wouldn't jar with the views, as brightly coloured flowers did – a vision of all-white which would harmonize.'

The nine-metre-by-seventeen-metre site, bordered on one side by a series of drawing room windows and on the other by a stone wall, was divided into three interlocking areas or 'rooms', all on a central axis lying parallel to the apartment. Thus as one moves from one room to the next, the views change accordingly, with one geometrically shaped space succeeding another, in an effect which greatly increases one's sense of the garden's scale. Individually treated with contrasting white-flowering varieties, the three spaces – one square, one oval and one rectangular – are unified by the use of grass as ground cover and dark, evergreen shrubs as background, some clipped into uniform architectural shapes and others left in their natural state.

Tall French windows lead from the main, off-white salon into the square garden. Edging the grassy enclosures and defining the area are beds planted with ivy and low clumps of *Rhododendron yakushimanum*, which bear clusters of bell-shaped pearly-white flowers, opening from pink buds in May. Their long, dark evergreen leaves form rounded domes which break the sharp angles of the building's façade, softening the transition between the garden and the pale stone wall. In May and June the creamy-white lacy flowers of a climbing hydrangea, *H. petiolaris* and the white star-like flowers of *Clematis montana* transform the evergreen curtain of ivy that covers the perimeter wall, continuing the colour theme from the white tulips and narcissi planted at random in the beds beneath.

A cream-coloured stone tread marks the entrance into the oval garden. Flanking it are groups of box clipped into fat balls and rounded clumps of snow-white flowering

Right, set against a backdrop of varying shades of green, tall white 'Glacier' Darwin tulips brighten the oval garden 'room'. Carefully clipped box flanking the steps that lead to the middle area adds a note of formality.

Far right, the wing covered in ivy was added by Mme Rochas to provide a salon from which to view the garden with its three 'rooms'.

The fresh green-and-white garden is shaded by the nineteenth-century house on one side and by towering horse chestnuts on another.

azaleas, which add a touch of formality with their geometric forms, while at the same time undermining it with their playful juxtaposition of different heights and volumes. From here curve two long beds, one banked against the building's façade and the other against the perimeter wall. Their graceful curves, which create a feeling of enclosure, contain the garden's main concentration of seasonal plantings.

In early spring the beds are edged with the common daisy, *Bellis perennis* 'Snow Ball', a perennial, treated here as an annual, which carpets the ground with hundreds of tiny white flowers. Raised above the white ground cover on slender sixty-centimetre-high stems are the large translucent blooms of dozens of 'Glacier' Darwin tulips, silhouetted against the dark evergreen foliage of *Choisya ternata*, which bears sweetly scented white flowers in April, and tall rhododendrons.

Trained along the top of the stone wall are the gnarled, twisted branches of a hardy wisteria, *W. floribunda* 'Longissima Alba', pruned over the years into gracefully leafy arches, which turn brilliant yellow in

with its exquisitely formed pure white double flowers, flushed with pink in bud, and *R.* x *alba* 'White Rose of York', the centuries-old Species rose with soft grey-green foliage and fragrant single or semi-double blooms, and 'Mme Plantier'.

By the autumn, when most of the flowering shrubs and perennials have produced their show of white blooms and the plane trees on the horizon are beginning to take on a tinge of yellow, the beds are replanted with densely massed dwarf white florist's chrysanthemums, *C. morifolium*. Bedded out annually, the chrysanthemums' showy, double flowers create a polka-dot effect against the dark evergreen background, and continue the garden's white theme through autumn and on until the winter frosts.

A second stone tread, again flanked by clipped balls of box announces the step up to the third, rectangular area of the garden, screened from the oval area by the lilacs and rhododendrons on one side, and on the other by a tall *Philadelphus coronarius*, which bears orange-blossom scented white cup-shaped flowers in summer. Shaded by a neighbouring horse chestnut, festooned with 'candles' in May, this dappled garden 'room' is simply planted, with dense ivy cloaking the stone wall's surface, and a two-metre-high clipped yew hedge screening out the next-door garden. As Mme Rochas explains, 'It was planned as an area for outdoor dining, and apart from the few times I've used it for that, it mainly serves as a cool retreat in the summer months.'

Inspired originally by English examples of gardens on the theme of a single colour, and of the concept of garden 'rooms', Hélène Rochas's garden is nevertheless suffused with a traditionally French perception of the relationship between house and garden. Subtly arranged within its evergreen framework, this all-white garden was designed to inspire changing moods, and to be appreciated as much from inside the apartment as from outside.

Above, the profusion of *Syringa villosa*, rhododendron blossoms and tulips creates a richness that lights up a corner of Hélène Rochas' green-and-white garden.

Left, adding a note of formality, small box bushes are clipped into round balls, contrasting with the natural growth all around.

autumn. The long white racemes of fragrant white flowers bloom in May, conveniently bridging the flowering seasons. Planted at the far corners are late-flowering white lilacs, *Syringa villosa*, which, with a dark-leaved Smirnow rhododendron, form a dense hedge between the oval and the rectangular gardens. After flowering, the lilacs are pruned to prevent them from shooting up too far above the wall and to promote flowering the following year. With the white-flowering rhododendrons they add height to the 'room', while adding a note of rural simplicity.

As the tulips fade they are succeeded by a large collection of old-fashioned white-flowering roses, which fill the beds throughout the summer. Mme Rochas chose old-fashioned varieties for their heady fragrance and their lax, arching habits of growth, which catch and hold the sunlight on summer afternoons. 'Old roses have always been my favourites,' she says, 'with their romantically feminine qualities that make the garden so delicately light and airy.' Of the hybrid perpetuals she selected the white-cupped 'Mabel Morrison', the recurrent white 'Candeur Lyonnaise', and the double pure-white 'Frau Karl Druschki', which she planted with the Damask, 'Mme Hardy',

24

A GARDEN OF MIRRORS

Mme Pierre Schlumberger
VIᵉ arrondissement

The Rue Férou in the *VIᵉ arrondissement* is like a secret passage linking the Place Saint-Sulpice with the Luxembourg Gardens. In this picturesque narrow cobbled street, lined with houses of the *ancien régime,* time seems to have stood still: Madame de la Fayette was born and died here in the seventeenth century, and little seems to have changed since. Halfway down, beneath the chestnut trees, a pair of eighteenth-century terracotta sphinxes flanks the courtyard entrance to the Hôtel de Luzy, the home of Madame Pierre Schlumberger.

The original seventeenth-century building, where D'Artagnan is supposed to have lived, was radically altered in the second half of the eighteenth century. The architect Marie-Joseph Peyre, who was responsible with Charles de Wailly for the neighbouring Théâtre de l'Odéon, in 1770 redesigned the *hôtel* complex in its current form. As it now stands the Hôtel de Luzy is an outstanding example of the neoclassical style that began to gain favour towards the end of Louis xv's reign and reached its full flowering under Louis xvi.

The *hôtel* is not named after one of its former owners, but rather after a former tenant, Dorothée Dorinville, who was given a lease to the house in perpetuity. During her time here, the celebrated actress, known at the Comédie Française by her stage name, Mademoiselle de Luzy, kindled passions in the breasts of large numbers of male admirers, including in 1772 the eighteen-year-old Duc de Talleyrand, a student at the Saint-Sulpice seminary nearby. From the Revolution to the middle of this century, the

Left, the *trompe l'oeil* wall with its three sets of mirrored French windows reflect the classical façade of the Hôtel de Luzy and also the centrally placed garden, apparently doubling it in size.

Previous page left, the Hôtel de Luzy's elegant, symmetrical garden façade: the decorative panels above the first-floor windows are attributed to Clodion.

Previous page right, in a corner of the garden white-flowering rhododendrons, impatiens and variegated ivies are planted to break the formal lines of the building's façade.

Right, stretching from the terrace to the *trompe l'oeil* wall the large, square lawn provides a lush green year-round feature to this garden of refined simplicity.

Below, a dark green wooden *étagère* set in a niche of the *trompe l'oeil* wall and planted with white-flowering petunias and impatiens emphasizes the air of formality while hanging tendrils of Virginia creeper and ivy add a softening touch of romanticism.

hôtel passed from hand to hand; neglected and abused, it settled into a state of steady decline from which it might never have recovered.

Fortunately in 1970 it was bought and saved by the late Pierre Schlumberger and

his wife, who have restored the *hôtel* and its garden to their former graceful elegance. With its interiors designed by Rybar and Daigre and its garden by Peter Coats, the *hôtel* is now an appropriate setting for an impressively eclectic collection of paintings, furniture and *objets d'art*. A great patron of contemporary art, Mme Schlumberger has created a unique environment in which works of various periods not only sit happily together, but also are displayed to perfection against the uncompromising neoclassicism of the eighteenth-century *hôtel*.

Harmony and balance are the hallmarks of the rectangular cobbled courtyard. Two of its sides are enclosed by the building's façades, and on the third, for the sake of symmetry and balance, is a *trompe l'oeil* imitation of the façade opposite. The chief decorative element on the façades is provided by terracotta panels above the first-floor windows, attributed to Clodion. Between the three arched windows of the ground-floor salon are two standard bay trees, *Laurus nobilis*, planted in contemporary versions of the *caisses de Versailles* originally designed for Louis XIV's exotic collection of pomegranates and orange and lemon trees. Then as now, the trees were sheltered in the *orangerie* during the winter and brought out to decorate the parterres in the warmer months. Decorative as they are, the boxes are also highly functional, and carefully designed for this peripatetic life. Raised on four corner posts for easy lifting, they have one side that opens on hinges to enable trees to be transplanted from one box to another. The white-painted wooden boxes in Mme Schlumberger's courtyard add a note of stately formality which foreshadows the garden beyond.

A seventeenth-century wing, the only surviving part of the original structure, houses the ground-floor library and runs at right angles to the central core of the *hôtel*. Linking the two is a room inspired by eighteenth-century garden pavilions, where pale green trellis-work frames hundreds of mirrored panels. A late eighteenth-century terracotta fountain supported by water nymphs stands in a niche, on axis with a pair of French windows opening on to the garden. In the mirrors a thousand tiny images of the room and the garden seem constantly to fragment and coalesce, to disappear into infinity and to take shape again, mingling interior and exterior views in a kaleidoscope of greenery and light.

The teasing distortions of scale and space are a fitting introduction to the elements of surprise and trickery employed outside. The garden, like the house, was conceived according to strict classical notions of geometric line and proportion, yet its cool formality has everywhere been either tempered or deliberately exaggerated by the use of theatrical effects. The play of scale and balance, of light and false perspective, already seen in the courtyard and the mirrored pavilion, here produce an overall atmosphere alive with the confrontation and resolution of two different eras: the harmony of classical order and calm is simultaneously ruptured and thrown into high relief by the careful introduction of irrational, romantic elements.

A procession of arched French windows leads out from the ground-floor reception rooms, and with the library wing defines two of the garden's four equal sides. On a wide travertine stone terrace running the length of the salons are two groups of black wrought-iron tables and cushioned armchairs which function as an outdoor extension to the reception rooms. Placed between the arches are dark green *caisses de Versailles* planted with large specimens of *Camellia japonica*. Their glossy deep-green foliage, silhouetted against the pale wall, heightens the impression of formality. When winter is over they also add a note of colour: 'There is no greater joy', says Madame Schlumberger, 'than when the camellias come into bloom in late February. Their pink flowers are such a

luxury in the greyness of early spring.' Protected from sudden frosts in winter by careful wrapping, and sheltered from the early morning sun, which can cause frostbite on the leaves, the precious trees have grown to a considerable size, and are a source of great pride to their owner.

At the other end of the garden, opposite the ground-floor salons, stands a three-dimensional single-storey false wall, complete with arched French windows and stone string courses. The Schlumbergers built this *trompe l'oeil* wall, an exact copy of the façade opposite, to balance the twenty-five-metre-square garden. The arched windows are mirrored to reflect the garden and create the illusion of greater space. When viewed from within the house, it has the air of another wing, as yet unexplored.

Two arched niches at either end of the *trompe l'oeil* wall contain wooden *étagères* conceived by Peter Coats. The stylized basket-like boxes, contemporary interpretations of French eighteenth-century designs, recall the fanciful engravings published by Georges-Louis Le Rouge in his *Détails des nouveaux jardins à la mode*, the album of plans for gardens, existing and imaginary, which was so great a source of inspiration in the late 1770s, and which encouraged the development of the *jardin à l'anglaise* style. The *étagères* here are filled in spring with white tulips and pansies, and in late summer they brim over with white impatiens and begonias. The Schlumbergers used only white-flowering varieties in the garden, as they felt that strong colours need a greater space to be appreciated. White also catches and holds the light in the garden's shadier areas, and complements the architectural composition of the *hôtel*.

Hidden behind the wall's *trompe l'oeil* stone string course are the roots of ivy and Virginia creeper, *Parthenocissus quinquefolia*, which have been trained to climb up and cover the rough stone surface of the wall of a neighbouring building, which rises above the false one. The five-storey-high green plane is transformed in autumn, when the Virginia creeper turns to shades of brilliant orange, scarlet and crimson. The creepers drape themselves over the string course and tumble down over the *trompe l'oeil* windows. Originally they were clipped more formally, to create green frames around the mirrored arches. Recently Mme Schlumberger has given them more freedom, so that festoons of ivy and Virginia creeper intertwined with each other now cascade down the wall, like garlands for a *fête galante*. Though they are still clipped to control their growth, they create a romantic, naturalistic effect, softening the severely architectural façade.

The fourth garden wall, opposite the library wing, has been planted exclusively with trained ivy: the odd tendril of Virginia creeper only becomes apparent in autumn, blazing scarlet against the rich green ivy. This wall of ivy, four storeys high, contrasts with the other three walls and harmonizes with the large central lawn. This perfect square of green, framed by the pale travertine stone path, and overlooked by the sheer, dark green wall, creates a graphic interplay of images throughout the year, the abstract geometric shapes and areas of colour having a soothing constancy during the cold grey winters. A narrow bed between the perimeter path and library wing is planted with the pale pink climbing rose 'New Dawn', underplanted in late spring with white impatiens.

The garden has no trees or shrubs, in order not to clutter the simplicity of the façades, which are officially classified as of outstanding historical and architectural merit. Ivy and Virginia creeper were a discreet and non-intrusive solution to the problem of covering the neighbouring walls which might otherwise interrupt views from the house.

The beautiful proportions of the neoclassical façades create a cool, formal atmosphere which is reflected in the way the garden is laid out. While the Hôtel de Luzy dates from

the time in French architectural history which saw a return to balance, order and symmetry, the garden also mirrors the movement that followed the return to classicism. In the age of romanticism, formal, geometric compositions were softened to accommodate new notions of the 'picturesque' and the romantic. Here, the *trompe l'oeil* wall, garlanded with ivy and Virginia creeper, recalls the ruined temple scenes painted by Hubert Robert, Louis XVI's garden designer. Mme Schlumberger's garden, at once formal and informal, unites classicism with romanticism; here order and fantasy co-exist, each throwing fascinating sidelights on the other.

On the stone terrace that runs the length of the Hôtel de Luzy's ground-floor salons Mme Schlumberger's prized camellias grow in contemporary versions of seventeenth-century *caisses de Versailles*. Beyond, the elegant trellis work, half-hidden by Virginia creeper, echoes the classical lines of the *hôtel particulier*.

25

A JARDIN
À L'ANGLAISE

M. and Mme Henry Pillsbury
VIIe arrondissement

Halfway down the busy Rue de Bac, flanked on either side by bustling local shops and cafés whose tables spill out on to the narrow pavement, stands a fine mid-eighteenth-century *porte-cochère*. The beautifully carved and painted doors are usually left open, to reveal glimpses of Judith and Henry Pillsbury's Paris garden.

Unlike so many gardens in the elegant Faubourg Saint-Germain, where the smallest hint of greenery is generally shut firmly away behind forbiddingly high walls or impenetrable-looking façades, the Pills-

burys' large garden gives itself away with telltale glimpses, clearly visible from the busy street, and is protected by little more than iron railings. Yet as you cross the cobbled courtyard to their delightfully informal garden, where nature is coaxed rather than controlled, you experience a strong sense of privacy, and even mystery.

Since the Pillsburys discovered it in 1974, the garden has developed and changed with Judith Pillsbury's growing passion for gardens and gardening, for which it has in turn provided the inspiration.

Right, the children's former sandpit has been transformed into a peaceful corner for retiring to in fine weather. Built on the foundations of what was once a stable, the area is planted with Japanese anemones, which flower in late summer.

Previous page left, some of the garden's main features are captured in this view across the cobbles and octagonal pond to the elevated courtyard beyond.

Previous page right, large clumps of plantain-lily hostas border the pond. Granite cobblestones taken from elsewhere in the garden were arranged around the pond by Michel Boulcourt.

The rectangular plot is unusual in plan, and quite different from the classic Parisian arrangement of three blocks – courtyard, building and garden – lying parallel to the street, and laid out so that one crosses the courtyard to reach the house, and the house to reach the garden. Here both the apartment and the garden are perpendicular to the street, with the courtyard on one side and an adjoining garden on the other. Thus the garden seems to gain in size, as the eye naturally travels on to include the neighbouring spaces. The illusion is compounded by the fact that the garden lies three metres below the level of the courtyard, so the eye is drawn upwards and outwards.

When the Pillsburys arrived there were some rusty old railings and a gate dividing the courtyard from the garden, with a flight of steps between the two levels. 'It wasn't really much of anything fifteen years ago; it looked more like an abandoned, overgrown country farm, with some gravel patches and

scattered, sad-looking shrubs,' says Judith Pillsbury. In one of the corners opposite the apartment stood some tumbledown stables, reached from the courtyard on one side by a narrow ramp. Privet, forsythia and laurel bushes were the extent of the planting, straggling in a tangled mass down the length of the garden, their dark shadows merging with the dense growth of ivy on the stone wall of a neighbouring building, over which the Pillsburys looked out.

The first thing they did was to replace the railings with tall, slender black-painted ones, similar to those that surround Parisian parks. They blocked off the steps at the courtyard level, and on them arranged terracotta pots planted with a variety of flowering plants, including brilliant violet-pink *streptocarpus*, Cape primrose, an assortment of fuchsias, impatiens and blue and white campanulas. These add colour and height to the space while at the same time camouflaging the steps and retaining wall.

Faced with this twelve-by-twenty metre plot, Judith Pillsbury sought all the advice and inspiration she could find: 'I first started reading anything I could find on gardens, since the space daunted me so.' She joined the British Royal Horticultural Society and became an assiduous visitor to their seasonal plant shows, including of course the Chelsea Flower Show in London each May; and she made studious tours of celebrated gardens throughout Europe, and particularly in England. Hidcote, Stourhead, Montacute, the wild and woodland gardens at Wisley, and above, all, Sissinghurst, all provided her with inspiration.

'I wanted to treat my space like an English country wild garden and, like Sissinghurst, to create a garden with different compartments and different seating areas. In many of the English gardens I've visited I was very interested in the use of the same plants employed repeatedly throughout the gardens, which gave an organized feeling to the spaces. It was four years ago, when we started to renovate the apartment and build an exterior staircase from the first floor to the garden below, that I decided really to have the garden re-structured to contain a number of different areas, like Sissinghurst.'

She asked the young French landscape architect, Michel Boulcourt, whose wide experience included a number of urban sites, to come and reorganize the garden space to include smaller, more intimate areas. Boulcourt began by grouping the different types of plants that Mrs Pillsbury had accumulated over the years, and designed areas within the rectangular space to correspond to the plants' various needs. In the natural enclosure formed by the stone foundations of the old stables the Pillsburys had constructed a sandpit for their children. This Boulcourt removed, at the same time replacing the sand and soil of the surrounding beds with a heavily compacted peat mixture. Using old railway sleepers (a rare sight in a French garden), he defined the edges of these

areas and built them up to create raised beds. The former sandpit was planted with *Cyclamen* x *atkinsii*, and from December to March is a carpet of delicate pink flowers. Rare Williams rhododendrons, *R. williamsianum*, whose evergreen kidney-shaped leaves and soft pink bell-shaped flowers, borne in April, need protection from frost, flourish in the rich, sheltered soil, interspersed with groups of pink-flowered *Hydrangea macrophylla* 'La France' and white-flowered *H. quercifolia*. This shady 'room', which the Pillsburys used for entertaining on warm summer evenings, has its own identity yet remains an integral part of the garden, as none of the shrubs is allowed to grow large enough to close the space off completely.

Beneath the ground-floor kitchen windows, at the foot of the steps, Boulcourt designed an octagonal pool, edged with large granite blocks which originally surrounded the gnarled old fig tree. Partly shading the pool's reflecting surface, the fig tree also

Bordering the house and edged with old railway sleepers, a rectangular bed of carmine impatiens and white-flowering tobacco plants provides vibrant splashes of colour.

Right, tall Easter lilies grow in the bed next to the house, their white blooms brightening the area.

Far right, Judith Pillsbury has grouped a variety of potted plants and arranged them on the old stone steps that lead from the courtyard to the garden

helps to obscure direct views into the garden from courtyard level. Around the rim of the pool, helping to soften its outlines and naturalize it with the garden's other planting, are moisture-loving plants such as large-leaved *Peltiphyllum peltatum* and *Hosta lancifolia*, transplanted from other parts of the garden, which thrive in the shady conditions. Behind the neat dark clumps of foliage box spheres of varying diameters are dotted up the bank that surrounds the courtyard, rising to the garden's only remaining group of spotted laurels, also clipped into rounded shapes. In winter, these distinctive evergreens provide an architectural backdrop, while in summer their geometric forms are softened and almost lost among the spreading perennials, which create the untamed, overgrown effect that Mrs Pillsbury wanted to achieve.

Beyond the old stables and the pool, both of which flank the courtyard, lies the central area of the garden. Here Boulcourt designed a symmetrically placed rectangular lawn framed by flowerbeds, edging both the lawn and the beds with more railway sleepers to create a natural effect: 'I use wood a lot in gardens: it reduces the sharpness of stone and harmonizes with foliage, while creating a softer, weathered look.'

On the house's garden façade *Clematis montana* clambers among the twisting stems and dense foliage of ivies and a Virginia creeper, mingling its subtle notes of blue with the vine's emerald-green leaves, before they take on their spectacular scarlet and crimson autumn colours. In summer tall stands of superb *Lilium regale*, underplanted with white nicotiana (tobacco plants) provide luminous highlights against the dense background foliage, while viburnums and hydrangeas add contrasting notes of green, creamy-white and pink to the beds.

Against the ivy-clad wall next door, Boulcourt massed a large collection of pink-flowering camellias, some as much as three metres tall, which had been scattered around

the garden. He combined their glossy evergreen foliage with Oregon grape, *Mahonia aquifolium*, and blue-green hollies, underplanted with snowdrops and early primulas, to create a bed which seems to add depth to the garden, as the light is reflected off the gleaming evergreen leaves.

At the far end of the lawn he planted huge banks of evergreen ferns, which enhance the woodland there. The delicate fronds enclose a bed of yellow archangel, *Lamium galeobdolon* 'variegatum', from which rises a towering sycamore tree. Early-flowering yellow crocuses add a note of contrasting brightness to the lamium's silver-flushed evergreen leaves, which provide useful ground cover, being hardy yet eye-catching.

Along the railings at the end of the garden are mounds of *Dicentra formosa*, 'Bountiful', the hybrid of *D. eximia* and *D. formosa* so often found in shady wild gardens. The pink heart-shaped flowers and feathery fern-like foliage are overhung by 'Excelsior' hybrid foxgloves in characteristic shades of pink, cream and white. Together they create a mixed palette, and add soft notes of colour to the evergreen background.

Another inspiration that Judith Pillsbury attributes to her English garden tours is the use of flowers in one colour range repeated throughout the garden and at every season of the year. She chose purples, blues and pinks for their subtlety and gentle harmonies within the garden's strong evergreen framework, adding accents of white and occasionally yellow to complement the mauve and blue tones. From the pale pinks of the *Peltiphyllum*, which arrive before the large leaves, to the gracefully arched racemes of the dicentras, the hostas' nodding lilac spikes and the soft pinks and creamy whites of the spreading hydrangeas, the garden blooms throughout the year amid its labyrinth of evergreens. Each season has a dash of yellow to highlight the effect: sweetly scented clusters of mahonia in winter, crocuses and primulas in spring, and frag-

rant lemon-yellow day lilies in summer. And in autumn, as the leaves on the surrounding trees turn to shades of ochre and the Virginia creeper deepens from crimson to bronze, the whole garden, with its many elements, seems to glow gold in the afternoon sunlight.

The discreetly domesticated wildness of the garden acts as a delightful counterbalance to its urban setting. The guiding principles of Judith Pillsbury and Michel Boulcourt, and many of the wild gardens and planting schemes that inspired them, were all derived ultimately from the ideas of William Robinson and Gertrude Jekyll. Starting with a strong framework of low-maintenance, exotic shrubs, they added subtle colour combinations with a few stronger accents to illumine the darker reaches. Their informal treatment, barely betraying the controlling hand of a gardener, has created a structure of varying areas at once flowing into each other and subtly differentiated. The wild garden, here created with so much loving care, is an increasingly important feature of the urban environment, transporting the visitor far away from the city, into the countryside and beyond. In this elusive world nature, freed from the shackles of formality and uniformity, presents its loveliest and most soothing aspect to the harassed city dweller.

Left, a yellow-flowering day-lily adds a touch of bright colour to the carefully cultivated green wilderness.

Far left, rather than planting dark-leaved ground cover such as *Vinca minor*, Judith Pillsbury and Michel Boulcourt used variegated lamium, whose silvery foliage catches the dappled light and brightens an otherwise dark corner.

26

A ROOFTOP RETREAT

Mme Andrée Putman
VIe arrondissement

Just a block away from the river Seine and the Pont Neuf Andrée Putman's New York-style loft and its terrace garden are hidden high up among the seventeenth- and eighteenth-century grey slated roofs of the *rive gauche*, in the heart of one of the most historic parts of the *VIe arrondissement*. With the same sure skill that she applies to her work as an interior designer, she has created a delightful and highly original roof garden. Reminiscent in some respects of the romantic cottage gardens of the Île de France region, and in others of the landscapes of Provence, the terrace is a unique juxtaposition of disparate elements, which together create an effect that is purely contemporary. Never one to shy away from mixing styles or periods – her design company reproduces 1920s and 30s furniture designs, and her living area contains objects as diverse as an eighteenth-century German grandfather clock with a case of engraved mirror-glass and chairs by Le Corbusier – Mme Putman has used her rooftop space to express her delight in eclecticism, coupled with a taste for severely monochromatic schemes.

Previous page left, running the length of the rooftop garden a wooden fence covered with the Bourbon rose 'Boule de Neige' and goat-leaf honeysuckle, *Lonicera caprifolium*, provide privacy without obscuring the bird's-eye view of Paris beyond. Below the fence, narrow beds are filled with hostas, lavender and rosemary.

Previous page right, over one hundred white rose bushes fill the rooftop, their heavily scented blooms creating a country-garden atmosphere all summer long.

Clusters of small pots planted with a large variety of herbs and dwarf alpine perennials emphasize the cottage-garden feel of this extraordinarily diverse garden.

The conservatory, used throughout the year as a peaceful retreat, offers views not only of the garden but also of the dramatic skyline of rooftops, garret windows and chimneypots.

Ten years ago she lived in the house next door to where she is today, feeling, as she says, like a character in Hitchcock's *Rear Window*. Her apartment was on the top floor of the fifteenth-century Hôtel d'Hercule (named after the tapestries and frescoes depicting the labours of Hercules that adorned its interiors), which towards the end of the following century was annexed by the Hôtel de Savoie-Nemours. By 1812 the latter, now known as the Hôtel Conflans-Carignan, had become the house of the *Journal de la Librairie*, and later in the nineteenth century, in the garden behind, an addition was built to accommodate the printers' expanding offices. For years Mme Putman had a bird's-eye view of the comings

and goings in the little factory, as the printing presses gave way to other businesses, until in the 1970s the concern then in occupation abruptly went bankrupt and the premises were hastily vacated. From her privileged position, Mme Putman was among the first to know that the space was up for sale, and she wasted no time. Here was a challenge and an opportunity she could not resist – to create both a dramatic living area and a showplace both for her work and for that of artists who have influenced her.

The building – the only such conversion in the area – is surrounded on all sides by much older houses. Where other gardens are bounded by walls or fences, Mme Putman's terrace has the Parisian roofscape as its backdrop – mansard roofs, garret windows and chimneypots forming a surreal landscape which would not be out of place on a film set, and which could certainly not have been better positioned for dramatic effect.

When Mme Putman began work on the loft, one of her first projects was to build a large conservatory at the top of the wide metal staircase that links the downstairs living area with the rooftop garden above. The glass-panelled room, furnished with a marble-top bistro table and late nineteenth-century wicker furniture, serves as a dining area throughout the year, with constant views of the garden outside. The pitched glass roof lends the space something of the air of a hothouse, tucked away in some corner of a country garden, an effect compounded by the lush plant growth within: pelargoniums, pure white azaleas, potted palms and trailing dark green *Stephanotis floribunda*, whose waxy white flowers perfume the air throughout the winter. 'I'm often up here in all kinds of weather,' says the owner, 'transported far away for a moment's peace.'

In planning the roof garden itself, her aim was to create a sense of total privacy without losing the feeling of complete openness, unhampered or obscured by overhanging

As part of Andrée Putman's one-colour planting scheme, white-flowering daisies grow profusely at the base of each of the garden's two trees.

trees or the shade of neighbouring buildings. She erected a high wooden fence around three sides of the garden, and planted against it. Underneath it, running the length of the rectangular space, she built a low raised brick bed which she filled with the Bourbon rose 'Boule de Neige'. Borne recurrently throughout the summer, the globe-shaped double snow-white blooms open from scarlet buds over the wooden fence. As Mme Putman remarks, 'In mid-June, when there are hundreds of white roses in bloom, the effect is more than spectacular.'

The bed is also planted with silver-grey perennials including silky grey-green wormwoods *Artemisia stelleriana* and *A. absinthium*, their feathery, aromatic foliage the perfect complement to the roses

above them. Twining among the rose stems is *Lonicera caprifolium*, goat-leaf honeysuckle, a European native which grows rampantly in all directions, and is covered from June onwards in whorls of fragrant creamy-white flowers. In June and July the double white flowers of *Philadelphus* 'Boule d'Argent' add their sweet orange scent to this jungle of flowering shrubs. Its loosely arched branches, free and uncontrolled, make it seem as if it were growing in its wild state in the country. 'Boule d'Argent' was introduced to France in 1894 by Lemoine and Sons, the French nursery responsible for so many flowering shrubs, including varieties of deutzia, weigela and syringa, as well as over twenty varieties of philadelphus.

At the other end of the garden, dense tufts

of old English lavender and rosemary spill over the edges of a raised square bed. A dark green ivy, clothing the wall behind, contrasts with their aromatic grey-green foliage and recalls for Mme Putman memories of her house in the south of France. In summer, when the lavender and rosemary bear their mauve and blue flowers among the rocks and gravel, this corner of the garden could almost be a rugged stone outcrop in Provence not a Parisian rockery.

Other features add elements of more classic French garden design: a clipped yew hedge, which adds further protection to the garden, and a magnolia and an oleaster, *Elaeagnus angustifolia*, grown as standards in large terracotta pots. With their long straight trunks and rounded tops they add echoes of much more formal schemes, while their foliage and flowers add yet another element to the garden's theme and variations on tones of silver, green and white. The magnolia's glossy dark evergreen leaves not only act as a foil to the blooms in late June, but also contrast beautifully with the willow-like grey-green leaves of the elaeagnus, which bears inconspicuous silvery-yellow flowers in June. In summer the trees are underplanted with mounds of white marguerites, and in autumn with off-white begonias.

Nearby a cluster of small pots planted with a large variety of herbs and dwarf alpine perennials, returns to the informal theme. Casually grouped and growing into one another at will, they add a cosy, cottage-garden feel to this extraordinarily diverse garden.

Paradoxically, in some respects Andrée Putman's garden is diametrically opposed to the simplicity and pure lines so often associated with the works of the artists of the 1920s and 30s which she espouses. Here, unconfined by straight lines or notions of geometric proportion, the garden flourishes amid the Parisian rooftops, like a small patch of nature accidentally left behind in the urban sprawl. But at the same time the colour scheme, elegantly and subtly restrained, with its cream and pastel shades, is a softer echo of the starkly monochromatic interior of the living area. And Mallet-Stevens canvas chairs with green-blue frames and the nineteenth-century *faux-bois* metal and cement benches and tables add a note of whimsy and set the keynote of – so important to Andrée Putman in her life and her work.

27

A COLOURFUL COURTYARD AND GARDEN

M. Valentine Abdy
XVIe arrondissement

Amid the leafy elegance and sedate rural charm of the *beau quartier* of Auteuil, on the south-western edge of the *XVIe arrondissement*, Valentine Abdy's garden comes as something of a colourful surprise. In the three years since his arrival he has transformed a 'dark and gloomy space' into a garden full of life and colour, skilfully laid out on several levels to take full advantage of the limited space available. In doing so he has freely adapted French ideas and techniques, taking the best from the nineteenth-century bedding designs that still flourish in

French public and private gardens alike. If his models have been traditional, however, his inspiration owes more to his own highly developed taste, and to an individualism – perhaps more British than French – which allows him cheerfully to ignore current fashions in garden colour while flouting conventional notions of design.

Auteuil, bordered on one side by the Seine and on the other by the Bois de Boulogne, has been famous for its gardens from as early as the seventeenth century. Then a small hamlet, it owed its increasingly noteworthy

Previous page left, viewed from the main salon, the bright colours of a bed of summer-flowering annuals are found again in the distance under the *Magnolia grandiflora* that Valentine Abdy discovered and transported from Naples.

Previous page right, the flower-filled patio continues the muticoloured theme of the garden and brightens the views from the apartment.

A massive group of vivid purple-flowering *Hydrangea macrophylla* add colour to the long stone wall that marks one boundary of Valentine Abdy's garden.

population to the fact that it lay conveniently on the road from Paris to Versailles. Some of the most glittering adornments of the Sun King's court, including Molière and Boileau-Despréaux, and later, Hubert Robert, built country houses on the banks of the river here, surrounding them with noble woods and avenues. One of the largest of these estates belonged to Nicolas Boileau-Despréaux, poet, critic and historiographer to Louis XIV, whose garden, renowned for its array of picturesque features and its arboretum containing many rare and exotic trees, proved a source of inspiration to many sonneteers of the day.

In the century and a half that followed Boileau-Despréaux's death in 1711 the estate changed hands several times, virtually doubling in size on each occasion; and in 1860, when the Chamber of Deputies passed a bill authorizing the annexation of twenty-four *communes* on the periphery of old Paris, it became part of Paris. The city itself now doubled in size and was divided into twenty *arrondissements*, and the densely wooded Boileau lands were crisscrossed with a network of private roads called, rather confus-

ingly, *villas*. Known today as the Hameau de Boileau, this area of narrow, winding chestnut-shaded lanes and elegant nineteenth-century houses still preserves a 'village' air. It is in this uniquely rural part of Paris, on the Villa Molitor, that Valentine Abdy has his apartment and garden.

Abdy's first concern in designing his garden was to create views that could be enjoyed from the salon windows, which run the length of the garden façade. He wanted, above all, a strong backdrop for the apartment's interiors, dynamic and full of interest, which would bring the ten-by-fifteen-metre plot to life. Built on to the salon at one end is a conservatory, used primarily as a dining area. A *Wisteria sinensis* twines round its iron railings, which frame the views into the garden from the interior.

When he arrived, the prospects seemed unpromising. Right in the middle of the garden stood a large, overgrown yew tree, entirely filling the central area and, as he says, 'terribly depressing to look at, although it divided me from my neighbours at the bottom of the garden.' On either side of the rectangular site were stone walls, two and a half metres high, allowing glimpses of neighbouring greenery at tree level, while blocking any views of the gardens behind. And at the far end, above an ivy-clad wall, rose a tall mansion block, revealed in its full glory when Abdy, after much hesitation, finally felled the forbidding-looking yew.

At basement level was built a brick-floored patio, walled on two sides by the house and conservatory. Hidden from view from the main rooms, it forms a private, enclosed courtyard for the basement rooms. Large terracotta pots planted in spring with purple rhododendrons and pink camellias continue the garden's colourful planting scheme. Here, in mid-May, when the rhododendrons are in full bloom, Adby underplants the evergreen shrubs with vivid impatiens, nicotiana, begonias, African mari-

The colourful bedding scheme cascades over the retaining walls of the patio, while the lower level itself is full of terracotta pots planted with bright red, pink and orange impatiens and hot-coloured camellias.

golds and zonal and ivy-leaved pelargoniums. The brilliant splashes of pink, orange and red, interspersed with white, flourish until the first frost in November.

On top of the patio's waist-high retaining wall is an L-shaped bed which forms the first of the garden's three levels. It is raked at an angle, so as to provide maximum impact when viewed from the salon, and as it slopes up to the garden's second level it also creates an illusion of size and depth.

Faced with a modest plot, Abdy employed various strategems to make it appear larger. When he first laid out the garden, he created three distinct levels, retreating to the shady far end. The three tiers, rising in succession against a darkened background, have the effect of making the garden seem both broader and longer.

On the first of the three levels, Abdy used the centuries-old practice of planting brightly coloured bedding plants to achieve vivid effects of contrasting colour and scale. Another ploy to increase the scale of the space was to echo the strong blocks of colour thus achieved in smaller clusters in the shady areas behind.

Not far from Abdy's garden, in the town of Boulogne-Billancourt, are les Serres d'Auteuil, the vast conservatories run by the city of Paris, which produce the thousands of tender annuals and half-hardy perennials that are used for bedding schemes in municipal gardens throughout Paris, from small public squares to the grandiose circular beds at the Rond-Point on the Champs-

Wisteria grows profusely over the conservatory and, next to it, the lower courtyard and apartment are surrounded by an L-shaped, sloping bed full of bedding plants.

Elysées and the rectangular plots of the Hôtel de Ville, designed by the artists Claude and François-Xavier Lalanne. They used vivid flowers and contrasting foliage plants to create short-lived, brilliantly coloured combinations, in a tradition which reached its apogée in the second half of the nineteenth century.

From 1860 Paris not only doubled in size, but it also changed radically in plan. Napoleon III commissioned Georges Haussmann to create a modern city with straight, tree-lined boulevards, large public parks and green squares. Haussmann gathered together a team of engineers, landscape architects and planners, including Jean-Charles Alphand, whose projects included the greenhouses at Auteuil, to supply the new squares

and bedding schemes. With his young assistant, Edouard André, Alphand was to create both public parks and private gardens throughout Europe in the latter years of the century. Together they did a great deal to promote the use of exotic plants in municipal settings, culminating in the intricate designs known as *mosaiculture*. In his treatise *L'Art des jardins*, published in 1879, André noted that the first major example of *mosaiculture* to catch the public's attention was at the Hamburg Horticultural Exhibition in 1869. Large beds, laid out in geometric designs of stars and circles, were planted with massed groups of brightly flowered plants, most of which originated in South and Central America and the Far East. Later the same year, at the Universal Exhibition in Paris, an enormous vase-shaped bed was planted with over 25,000 plants. Generally the beds were round or oval in shape, and slightly raised in the centre in order to be seen at best advantage from a distance. Called *corbeilles*, or baskets, they were like giant multi-coloured bouquets of flowers and variegated foliage, constantly renewed as the blooms faded.

On a much smaller scale and without any rigidly geometric layout, this was the effect that M. Abdy strove to create. In designing the rectangular bed, he relied on his gardener, M. Deboucoln, to devise a planting programme to fill the space with brightly coloured flowers through all the seasons. Twice a year, in mid-December and in mid-May, M. Deboucoln arrives with crates full of bedding plants. With the exception of a few that Abdy will not allow in his beds – including tulips – M. Deboucoln is free to compose his own designs, as long as they produce a broad spectrum of strong colours.

The spring-flowering scheme, bedded out by 15 December each year, contains a large collection of *Hyacinthus orientalis*, the florist's common hyacinth, including the white 'Edelweiss', the blue 'Ostara', the red 'Tubergen's Scarlet', and the shell-pink 'Lady Derby'. Massed by colour, they are underplanted with the dwarf primroses, *Primula allionii* and *Primula auricula*, and interspersed with the groups are tufted pansies, *Viola* x *wittrockiana*, *Viola cornuta* and Swiss Giant varieties. Perpetual-flowering stocks and Virginian cowslips, *Mertensia virginica*, add height.

In May M. Deboucoln returns to fill the beds with massed plantings of exotics which bloom throughout the summer and autumn. Brilliant scarlet and orange South African geraniums, *Pelargonium quercifolium* and *P. graveolens*, contrast with the creams and deep pinks of the Brazilian *Begonia semperflorens*, *Ageratum houstonianum* 'Tall Blue' and 'Fairy Pink', the Mexican annual with heart-shaped leaves, complement the strong palette of colours, which also includes deep orange *Zinnia angustifolia*. Also from Mexico are deep purple *Fuchsia fulgens*, staked so that they arch over the other plants, lending the bed an airy grace. By midsummer the bed is a dazzling patchwork of vivid colours, easily eclipsing the more subtle and muted

colour schemes of other Parisian gardens.

Behind this bed is a deep green rectangular strip which forms the second level. Leading from the conservatory steps to a stone-flagged seating area on the opposite side of the garden, this narrow grass path marks the boundary between the bedding area and the raised far end. A low brick retaining wall runs the length of this highest level, its continuous line broken only by a small grove of flame-red zonal pelargoniums cascading over it.

When travelling in southern Italy on one occasion, M. Abdy found four large *Magnolia grandiflora*, each over six metres tall, and clipped as standards. After a considerable amount of organization and at great expense, he had them shipped to Paris and planted at the far end of the garden. With their height and evergreen foliage they help to screen the building behind, and because of their unusual shape, the area beneath them was light enough for underplanting. The tall, straight trunks, spaced irregularly, with the tallest of the four in the foreground, seem to recede into an illusory distance. To increase this exaggerated feeling of depth, Abdy planted bright pink impatiens in a narrow strip at the foot of the ivy-covered wall, thus highlighting the edge of the garden.

Hidden in a far corner, under the canopy of neighbouring chestnut trees, a small garden shed is completely shrouded in ivy. Placed in front is a white-painted wooden bench which, like the strong-coloured, massed impatiens or pelargoniums, lights up the dark corner. A fragment of a giant terracotta flame burns brightly as a fanciful addition to the glowing colour scheme.

M. Abdy's garden, full of exuberance and vitality, transcends the nineteenth-century tradition to which it is heir. Confined within the placid expanse of green grass and sober foliage is a garden bursting with life and colour, which is perhaps the source as well as the expression of its owner's dynamic personality.

Down one side of the garden a grass path leads from the apartment's conservatory to the shaded seating area. A low brick retaining wall with an eye-catching terracotta flame sculpture at its far end marks the highest of the garden's three levels.

28

A Trellised Garden

M. François Catroux

VIe arrondissement

The Rue de Condé lies in the heart of the Odéon *quartier* of the *VIe arrondissement*. The street was originally built in 1520, when it ran across the vineyards that dotted the slope of the hill. With the construction of Marie de Médicis' Palais du Luxembourg by Salomon de Brosse, begun in 1615, it witnessed a great influx of nobles and princely families, notably the Condés who bought and enlarged a house in 1612, and after whom the street was subsequently named. The *quartier* underwent massive changes in 1773 when Louis XV bought the vast Condé *hôtel* and

gardens and demolished them to make room for a new theatre to house the Comédie Française. In 1779, Louis XVI moved the site of the theatre to a higher part of the Condé property, across the street from the Luxembourg so that ' … our subjects, before entering or leaving a performance at the Comédie Française, will be able to have a promenade in the Jardin du Luxembourg.' The design of the Théâtre de l'Odéon, as the theatre was called, was entrusted to the team of Peyre and De Wailly, and it opened its doors three years later. The theatre en-

Opposite, behind the garden table and against the trellis wall lies a bed bursting with evergreen shrubs such as aucubas and viburnums, with white-flowering impatiens adding dashes of colour.

Previous page left, the focal point of this secluded garden is the pool surrounded by ivy, its central, isolated position catching the eye immediately. Beyond, in the shade of the tall, ivy-covered trellis, the fresh white umbrella of the garden table contrasts simply yet effectively with the surrounding foliage.

Previous page right, echoing the formal yet whimsical air of the clipped box at the garden's entrance, two more carefully shaped balls stand at the edge of the pool.

couraged new building in the area, much of which was influenced by its neoclassical design.

The day François Catroux discovered there was an apartment available in the Rue de Condé in the Hôtel de Quatrenière de Quincy, dating from the late eighteenth century, he decided to take it for two reasons: he loved the neoclassical lines of the architecture and the intimacy of the garden. As one of France's leading interior designers, M. Catroux was too well aware of the potential of the ninety-square-metre space to be able to resist it. By using it as an outside living room he could effectively create an extension to the eighteenth-century apartment. Thus, after completely reorganizing the interiors around his unique collection of furniture and *objets d'art*, M. Catroux asked the landscape designer Jean-Marie Prévosteau to rework the garden. Together they worked out a clear, simple design, incorporating as much greenery as possible throughout the year, while at the same time allowing sufficient space for entertaining on a grand scale.

'The garden had already been redesigned twice before with very poor results,' recalls M. Catroux, 'so I told Jean-Marie I didn't want any plants in the garden that couldn't be found in any public park in Paris.' Using the nearby Jardin du Luxembourg as a guide to the art of the possible and indication of the types of plants M. Catroux had in mind, M. Prévosteau drew up a list of selected hardy evergreen shrubs and annual planting schemes, resolutely resisting any temptation to include the exotic and subtropical plants which he knew would be doomed to failure.

On entering the apartment through the front door the visitor is met with a view of the garden framed by the French windows. These open on to a sort of low balcony from which a few steps lead down into the garden. On the balcony, which acts as a viewing platform for the garden, M. Prévosteau simply mixed ivy and Virginia creeper, *Par-*

thenocissus tricuspidata, which intertwine with each other around the iron balustrade. In autumn, when the Virginia creeper undergoes its dramatic colour change, the two plants weave a breathtaking tapestry of brilliant scarlet and rich dark green, clearly visible from inside the apartment as well as outside. Placed on the balcony and on each step are spheres of box grown in small terracotta pots, which in their elegant simplicity are an appropriate introduction to the garden.

The square space is enclosed on two sides by the *hôtel*'s neoclassical façades, and on the other two by the stone walls of the neighbouring buildings, one of which is completely covered for all of its five storeys with a dense curtain of ivy. This undulating deep green surface, reflecting the sunlight and creating constantly changing patterns of light and shade, makes a superb year-round backdrop for the garden. Ivy has also been trained up the other walls, which have been covered with trellising, the wall of M. Catroux's apartment being distinguished by a smaller diagonal grid. By day, the fronds of ivy form a delicate counterpoint to the diagonal lines and white walls, increasing the sense of depth in the garden. By night, in the flickering light of large torches attached to the walls, the effect is most dramatic.

From his professional experience M. Catroux had learned the importance of creating a dominant element to act as a focal point in the small garden and to unify the composition. The obvious choice was an already existing central pool and fountain, three metres in diameter, and yet it needed something more if its impact was to be strong enough. His simple and ingenious solution was to cover the low brick rim with ivy, which now frames the water and cascades down over the gravel, somehow endorsing the pool with something of the mystery and romance of an ancient well or natural spring.

Curving sinuously around the pool, at the foot of the stone wall, is a wide perimeter

bed, designed to be viewed from the apartment windows, and stocked with plants chosen for their year-round interest. Dotted at intervals along the edge of the bed are large spheres of box, making allusion to the smaller ones on the steps and at the edge of the pool. Their tiny, neatly clipped foliage contrasts with the long, slender, slightly rumpled foliage of *Viburnum rhytidophyllum* and the aromatic leaves of *Choisya ternata*, Mexican orange, which in late spring is covered with fragrant clusters of white flowers. The more difficult shady spots are filled by the ever-tolerant *Aucuba japonica*, which, with its evergreen spotted leaves and scarlet berris in winter, has saved many an otherwise hopeless-seeming urban site.

In the corner of the two neighbouring stone walls is a large Dexter hybrid rhododendron, 'Scintillation', with dense, evergreen foliage and lavender-pink flowers. Underneath it, and here and there throughout the garden, are clumps of white impatiens, adding touches of light in dark corners and outlining the silhouettes of the evergreen shrubs. A further note of white is added in midsummer by the fragrant flowers of *Hosta plantaginea*, rising from mounds of large ribbed oval leaves. Another white flowering perennial in the garden is *Acanthus mollis*, planted in a small ivy bed beneath the steps. With its handsome, distinctive leaves and tall flower spikes it makes a striking feature and creates interesting contrasts with the other plants. Standing just outside the apartment windows, and planted near the building for extra protection, are pillar-shaped camellias, used to add a note of formality in the manner of clipped box or yew in classical French gardens. From early spring they are covered with waxy white blooms, and in late spring they are underplanted with cushions of white impatiens.

M. Prévosteau's strategy for dealing with the limitations so often found in urban sites was to narrow down the varieties of plants used, and then to emphasize and play on the differences in their overall shape and leaf form. While they were chosen basically for their structure, many of them also add seasonal interest during their flowering periods. And, most importantly for M. Catroux, when viewed from inside the garden forms a lush backdrop, with its array of every shade of green silhouetted against the trellised walls. M. Catroux uses the garden whenever possible for entertaining, with conversation punctuated by the trickle of the fountain. In colder weather, he simply lights the bamboo torches, which highlight the reflective surfaces of the leaves and the rippling water and cast dramatic shadows. M. Catroux, with the help of M. Prévosteau, has played on the subtle effects of light, colour and form to create a simple and relaxed atmosphere, spiced with small touches of surprise to keep his interest – and that of his guests – constantly alive.

Right, at the garden's entrance and against a backdrop of Virginia creeper, carefully arranged terracotta pots planted with clipped box add a formal yet slightly whimsical touch.

Leading from M. Catroux's apartment are steps banked by a bed full of *Acanthus mollis* and contrasting, smaller-leaved ivies.

29

A PEACEFUL COTTAGE GARDEN

Mlle Carole Weisweiller
XVIe arrondissement

After two years of searching Paris for a house with a plot of land that could be turned into something resembling a garden, Carole Weisweiller found what she was looking for: a little house and garden peacefully ensconced in a narrow, private cul-de-sac hidden behind the extremely grand and equally congested Avenue Foch. Like a number of small houses in the area, it is concealed among the opulent stone façades that are typical of the *XVIe arrondissement*. Unlike the others, however, it was woefully neglected: it had lots of potential, but very little

else. Undeterred, and with the help of stalwart friends who have rallied round, Mlle Weisweiller has turned the crumbling house and its patch of rubble into a delightfully pretty little enclave, imbued with its own particular charm.

The house sits at the end of a garden which had been partially built over: first in the late nineteenth century, when a small two-roomed lodge was constructed in it, and then in the mid-1930s, when a sculptor's studio was built on the street side. The crazily gnarled and twisted limbs of a magnificent

The cottage atmosphere is heightened by the twisting *Parthenocissus* that winds its way along the house façade and around the front door. 'I was heartbroken when the workmen cut the original creeper, but now, in just a few years, this one has taken over completely,' says Mlle Weisweiller.

Camellias, lavender, pansies and primroses, along with Easter lilies make up the varied plantings in a garden filled with the owner's favourite flowers.

Previous page left, the narrow terrace, planted with potted shrubs, flowering trees and rows of vegetables, is used as an extension of the conservatory-dining-room in fine weather.

Previous page right, pale pink roses and white impatiens fill the narrow bed that borders the stone terrace.

fig tree cast their baroque shadow on the south-facing wall, and rising above the general rubble, in the shade of a neighbouring building, a sycamore struggled desperately for light. A tapestry of Virginia creeper and ivy hung from the adjacent six-storey wall and engulfed a large part of the house façade. But amid the crumbling plaster and general greyness of the scene, Mlle Weisweiller was struck by the romance of the little house.

Some time later, when it was covered in a thick layer of dust as workmen tore the place apart, it occurred to her that it would probably have been easier and cheaper had she simply pulled it down and started anew. After Antoine Jouve, an architect and family friend, had supervised the virtual rebuilding of the entire house, another friend, the Parisian interior designer François-Joseph Graff, helped to arrange Mlle Weisweiller's miscellaneous collection of late nineteenth-century furniture and *objets d'art* in the six-room house. He also designed a *jardin d'hiver* to incorporate her array of turn-of-the-century ceramic tiles decorated with bamboo and ivy motifs. This conservatory addition, which projects into the garden space, serves as a dining room. Like a miniature version of Princesse Mathilde's spectacular Parisian *jardin d'hiver*-cum-dining room of the 1860s, complete with flowerbeds, mature trees and a fountain, this little room is filled with cyclamens, vivid azaleas and brilliant red poinsettias. Their exotic colours, the richly patterned tiles and the elegant fronds of a collection of parlour palms together create a scene of *fin-de-siècle* lushness.

A wide green-painted iron gate screens the garden from the street. Within, pale pea gravel covers the small forecourt, originally designed as a car-parking area, but now incorporated as part of the approach to the garden and house. To avoid the risk of this area presenting a rather gloomy outlook from the first-floor windows, Mlle Weisweiller filled it with strong colour combinations.

Terracotta pots and troughs, some decorated with scroll designs or lions' heads, border the small space, and are planted with seasonal flowers: deep purple heather in early winter, to be followed by startling yellow and mauve crocuses in spring. Pink and red Darwin tulips then give place to glowing red and white pelargoniums and begonias in summer and autumn, so that throughout the seasons this apparently unpromising area is always a colourful introduction to the garden.

A flourishing Smirnow rhododendron, bearing lavender-pink flowers in June, shades the short flight of brick steps that leads down to the main garden level. Mlle Weisweiller solves the problem of providing the acid soil it requires by growing it in a large Tuscan terracotta pot, decorated with swags of garlanded fruit and flowers. To the right of the steps is the small building that was once the *concierge*'s lodge and now serves as the offices for the owner's documentary film production company. Both it and the house are painted a creamy-pink, with the door and window surrounds picked out in white, and green doors and shutters that call to mind Monet's pink and green house at Giverny. The Impressionists were not the inspiration for Mme Weisweiller's choice of colour scheme, for (as with Monet's house, painted by previous owners to remind them of their native Guadaloupe), in choosing her colours she hoped to recapture the atmosphere of the Mediterranean, and especially of her beloved Camargue.

Monet's garden, too, finds some parallels here. He filled the beds at Giverny with a riotous profusion of colour and form, and by disregarding the orthodox rules of planting (to the chagrin of his Norman gardener, M. Breuil) produced an overwhelming succession of flowers which seemed to become ever more luxuriant as the summer progressed. In this garden some of the same notions are apparent.

From the semicircular gravel forecourt in

Mlle Weisweiller had hoped that the lawn would be the scene of many afternoon picnics. Several wet summers, however, have dashed her plans and she realizes she must replant the area with something more resistant to rain. In early spring the small garden is scented with *Magnolia stellata*, which rises in the corner of the small bed.

The path leading to the front door is edged with dwarf box, recalling a French classicism whose formality contrasts with the rest of the garden.

front of the lodge, a path runs round the garden to the house. Edged in the customary French dwarf box, it is bordered on one side by flowerbeds reaching to the surrounding walls, and on the other by a central, pocket-sized lawn. In planning the space, Mlle Weisweiller longed to have an area of grass so that on long hot summer days she and her friends could have picnics there. The realities of recent rainy summers have given her second thoughts, however, and she is now investigating the different possibilities for replacing the frequently waterlogged grass. But for the moment it remains.

One of the first things she did in the garden was to plant thickets of fishpole bamboo, *Phyllostachys aurea*, to hide the neighbour-ing studio's grey stone walls. The tall shoots now jostle for space, arching gracefully over one side of the path, underplanted with clumps of the lesser periwinkle, *Vinca minor*, which adds a note of dark-leafed contrast to the bamboo's golden-green foliage. Peri-winkles were also originally planted under the sprawling fig tree which engulfs the bed running the length of the path down to the house. Ivy has since replaced it as shady ground cover because of its fast-growing properties. In late spring the narrow plot is bedded out with stark white impatiens, with the odd touch of vibrant pink. Providing ideal shade for them, the fig tree at this time of year seems to emerge from a glowing pink and white cloud.

The long-suffering sycamore on the other side of the garden was severely cut back to allow views of the garden from the *jardin d'hiver*. Beneath it were underplanted *Spiraea thunbergii*, lilies of the valley, which bear their clusters of small white flowers in March and April, more ivy ground cover, and a large rhododendron, *R. catawbiense*, which in June brightens up the shady corner with its vivid lilac blooms. The six-storey wall that abuts the area and rises parallel to one side of the *jardin d'hiver* was already veiled with Virginia creeper; however, as work progressed on the conservatory addition, an over-enthusiastic workman severed the vine's thick trunk. Trying to find the quick-est remedy for this tragedy, Mlle Weisweiller had long strands of ivy planted, which she then attached to the wall as though it had been there for years. Sadly the two Virginia creepers that frame the house's front door suffered the same fate, yet in both cases new shoots appeared the following year.

A flagged terrace in front of the house is separated from the garden by a three-foot-high brick wall. A bed beneath it is massed with yellow and red primulas, deep blue French lavender, pure white Easter lilies, a half-hardy species whose blooms spread their intoxicating perfume in July and

August, and shell-pink azaleas. Together they create a dazzling display of colour against a background of the many different textures and tones of the foliage. As at Giverny, where planting was planned so that not a speck of earth should be revealed, this bed fairly bursts with a wide variety of annuals, perennials, bulbs and flowering shrubs. Whenever a bare spot does appear, Mlle Weisweiller is at hand, perhaps with wild strawberries, variegated petunias or miniature dahlias. Dwarf crab apples planted in glazed Provençal pots sit on top of the wall underplanted with heather. This Mlle Weisweiller first planted in plastic bags containing acidic soil before placing it around the crab apples, thus satisfying the soil requirements of both.

Cement troughs contain the lilliputian vegetable garden. Staked tomatoes are flanked by climbing peas and coriander. Basil, chives, and parsely sprout in tiny rows amongst leafy Butternut and Romaine lettuces, adding to the house's country air.

From the soft-pink geraniums and crimson fuchsias to the delicately fragrant magnolia, *M. stellata*, that perfumes the early spring air, this little garden has a rare and very personal charm, very far removed from the imposing grandeur of the Avenue Foch.

Seen from the courtyard entrance of Carole Weisweiller's cottage, the multitude of potted annuals and climbing creeper bring a rural air to this small city garden.

30

A GRANITE-COBBLED COURTYARD

VIe arrondissement

While this granite-cobbled courtyard, has no pretentions towards being a luxuriant expanse of greenery, unlike many other such courtyards in Paris, for the many residents of the whitewashed buildings that overlook this secluded spot, the pleasures and satisfaction it affords are as great. While more traditional Parisian gardens, safely hidden behind high walls, are for the enjoyment of a privileged few, a courtyard like this is a valuable amenity for everyone in the vicinity, for all may benefit from its peace and charm.

It has a timeless quality, undisturbed by any brash intrusions, which allows the imagination to roam freely over past seasons and centuries. Framed by a pair of late eighteenth-century façades, with simple architectural lines and modest decorative detailing, the space seems for generations to have marked the passing seasons just as it does now.

Dominating the courtyard is a tall cherry tree, *Prunus avium*, which softens the lines of the architecture and transforms the enclosed area in early spring, when it is covered with white blossoms. Within a fortnight the cobblestones will be flecked with tiny white petals like confetti, and the blossom will give way to the leafy canopy that shades the courtyard throughout the summer. At the other end of the courtyard is a crab apple, which follows the cherry into blossom. Rising from an asymmetrical pillow of ivy, the crab apple too, once its delicate pink blossom is over, will contribute to the cool, shady atmosphere.

In winter and early spring the whitewashed façades reflect the light, bouncing it back and forth. This effect diminishes as the year progresses and more and more foliage grows up to soften and filter the light. As the crab apple comes into blossom, so dark purple-black Darwin tulips, planted in low troughs, unfurl their petals to create a striking and slightly menacing contrast with the whitewashed walls.

Among the patch of ivy that spreads over the granite blocks are dense clumps of perennial *Bergenia cordifolia*, which send up their spikes of mauve-pink flowers in March and April. They flourish in this cool, moist corner, and their spreading leaves seem to engulf the surrounding foliage. A sycamore sapling rises above, while the fronds of small scented ferns furl below.

By mid-May a 'Duke of York' rhododendron is covered with a magnificent display of mauve-purple scented blossoms, followed by the paler pink blooms of *R.* 'Scintillation'. The dark matt rhododendron foliage and the ivy patch are the courtyard's only touches of green in winter, yet even then the space seems full of life, as the twisted tree branches cast contorted shadows on the whitewashed walls and the uneven surface of the cobblestones, gleaming after rain. An old pump, a relic of the time before piped water, adds a touch of nostalgia, but its practical purpose is now served by a tap in the opposite corner. Between them, against the wall, are two old-fashioned Bourbon roses, 'Mme Ernst Calvat' and 'Louise Odier', which bear large

pink blooms recurrently throughout the season. In spring Chinese pots flanking the rose trough contain enormous hydrangeas, *H. macrophylla*, to be replaced towards midsummer by pale impatiens, which spill over the rim of the pots to brighten the shady courtyard.

The courtyard is tended by a few dedicated tenants, with no-one to lay down rules or draw up plans. Instead, its charming atmosphere has evolved piecemeal over the years, as each occupant has added his or her particular favourite to the scheme. In this rather haphazard way it has become a true community garden, where people meet to share advice and opinions, on the pretext of tending the plants.

The charm of this space is quintessentially French, an incongruous yet harmonious mixture of cool, restrained classicism, with soft colour and greenery to temper its severity, and an amiable atmosphere of *laissez-faire* to undermine its authority. Delightful as it is, it is an atmosphere that can be neither produced nor imitated by trying, for it has evolved in response to particular conditions and the characters of particular individuals which perhaps are only to be found in Paris.

BIBLIOGRAPHY

Adams, William Howard, *The French Garden 1500–1800*, George Braziller, New York, 1979

Fouquier, M. and Duchêne, A., *Des Divers Styles de Jardins*, Librairie Emile-Paul, Paris, 1914

Ganay, Ernest de, *Les Jardins de France*, Librairie Larousse, Paris, 1949
André Le Nostre, Editions Vincent Fréal, Paris, 1962

Gothein, Marie Luise, *A History of Garden Art*, trans. Mrs Archer-Hind, J. M. Dent, London, 1928

Hazelhurst, F. Hamilton, *Gardens of Illusion: The Genius of André Le Nostre*, Vanderbilt University Press, Nashville, 1980

Hénard, Robert and Fauchier-Magnan, A., *L'Hôtel Lambert*, Librairie Emile-Paul, Paris

Henderson, Marge and Wilkinson, Libby (eds.), *The House of Boughs*, Viking Penguin Inc., New York, 1985

Hillairet, Jacques, *Dictionnaire Historique; Des Rues de Paris*, vols. I and II, Les Editions de Minuit, Paris, 1963

Johnson, Hugh, *The Principles of Gardening*, Mitchell Beazley, London, 1979

Jones, Barbara, *Follies and Grottoes*, Constable, London, 1979

Lavedan, Pierre, *French Architecture*, Penguin, London, 1956

Lévêque, Jean-Jacques, *Jardins de Paris*, Hachette, Paris, 1982

Lloyd, Christopher, *The Well Chosen Garden*, Harper and Row, New York, 1984

Mollet, André, *Le Jardin de Plaisir*, Stockholm, 1651, new edn., Editions du Moniteur, Paris, 1981

Morse, Harriet K., *Gardening in the Shade*, Timber Press, Portland, 1982

Page, Russell, *The Education of a Gardener*, Collins, London, 1962

Pereire, A. and Van Zuylen, G., *Private Gardens of France*, Weidenfeld & Nicolson, London, 1983

Rouge, George Louis Le, *Details de Nouveaux Jardins à la Mode*, Paris, 1776–87

Schenck, George, *The Complete Shade Gardener*, Houghton Mifflin, Boston, 1984

Stuart Thomas, Graham, *Plants for Ground Cover*, new edn., J. M. Dent, London, 1984
Perennial Garden Plants, 2nd edn., J. M. Dent, London, 1982
Colour in the Winter Garden, 3rd rev. edn., J. M. Dent, London, 1984

Veyrier, Henri, *Le Faubourg Saint-Germain*, Editions Henri Veyrier, Paris, 1987
Chaillot, Passy, Auteuil, Le Bois de Boulogne, Editions Henri Veyrier, Paris, 1988

Wiebenson, Dora, *The Picturesque Garden in France*, Princeton University Press, Princeton, 1978

Wilder, Louise Beebe, *The Fragrant Garden: A Book About Sweet Scented Flowers and Leaves*, rev. edn., Dover Publications, New York, 1974

ACKNOWLEDGEMENTS

The author wishes to extend thanks to the owners and gardeners of the properties illustrated, whose generosity and kindness made this book possible, and also to the following people for their help: Joy Hendriks, Lord Weidenfeld, Michael Dover and Lesley Baxter from Weidenfeld and Nicolson, Kristen van Real, Gay Gassmann, Marie-Paule Pellé, Samia Saouma, Sandra Babeanu, Philippe Bouchney, Mattia Bonetti, Marian McEvoy, Carolina Estrada, Robert Couturier, the Musée de Blérancourt, where a large part of the text was written, and Konstantin Kakanias for his support through to the end.

FRENCH GLOSSARY

allée lane or path.

ancien régiem the political and social system that existed in France before the Revolution in 1789, now used to describe a former or superseded system.

arrondissements the twenty municipal districts or administrative sub-divisions of Paris.

atelier studio or workshop.

beau quartier the affluent area of a town or city.

boiserie wainscoting or panelling; usually applied to seventeenth- and eighteenth-century panelling elaborately decorated with shallow-relief carvings.

bouquetier usually flower seller or vase for flowers; also used as another term for *parterre* (see below).

butte mound or hillock.

caisses de Versailles decorative, portable flower boxes originally designed for Louis XIV's plant collection. One side of the box opens on hinges, enabling plants to be transplanted easily.

commune town, village.

corbeille basket, or ornament carved in the shape of a basket.

cour d'honneur main courtyard

département administrative division. France is divided into ninety-five such regions.

étagère stand with open shelves for displaying ornaments or plants.

fabrique usually factory or manufacture; also folly.

faux-boix imitation wood.

femme d'esprit woman of wit and learning.

fête fair, celebration, feast, holiday, saint's day.

fête champêtre garden party, picnic or similar outdoor entertainment.

fête galante as above; from the early eighteenth century, figures in a pastoral setting was a popular subject among French painters such as Watteau.

fin de siècle of or relating to the end of the nineteenth century when traditional social, moral and artistic values were in transition.

genre pittoresque ornate style of painting.

hôtel large building, hotel.

hôtel particulier private mansion.

jardin à la française formal garden.

jardin à l'anglaise landscape garden.

jardin de curé presbytery garden.

jardin d'hiver winter garden.

jardinière ornamental pot or trough for plants.

marais marsh, swamp.

miroir d'eau large pond used in classical French gardens for its reflective properties.

monument historique ancient monument, historic building.

mosaiculture intricate style of garden design in which beds were laid out in geometric patterns and planted 'mosaic-style' with massed groups of brightly flowering plants.

parterre level space, usually adjacent to main house, laid out in low, symmetrical patterns of beds and flowers.

parterre de broderie parterre whose designs comprised highly stylized scroll-shaped borders between which were planted a wide variety of exotic plants.

paysagiste landscape gardener.

pointilliste technique of painting, imposing dots of unmixed colour on a white ground, which fuse when viewed from a distance.

porte à voussure arched entrance.

porte-cochère large, covered carriage entrance into a courtyard.

potager kitchen or vegetable garden.

préfet chief administrator.

quartier district, area, neighbourhood.

rive gauche Left Bank, in Paris noted for its artistic and intellectual life.

salon reception room; also an informal gathering of intellectuals.

tapis vert green carpet or ground cover, baize.

trompe l'oeil 'deception of the eye'; a decoration which gives a convincing illusion of reality.

tuileries tilery, kiln; also a palace and gardens in Paris.

villa avenue, way.

SELECTED PLANT GLOSSARY

Acanthus mollis herbaceous perennial; height 1 m; glossy ovate leaves, white and purple flowers in July and August.

Acer campestre hedge maple; height 5–6 m; mid-green five-lobed leaves turning yellow in autumn.

A. palmatum Japanese maple; height up to 5 m; pale to mid-green leaves; parent of a number of forms.

A. platanoides Norway maple; height 10–12 m; bright green leaves turning yellow in autumn.

Aconitum napellus monkshood; height 1 m; dark green deeply cut leaves, violet-blue flowers in August and September.

Aesculus × carnea red horse chestnut; deciduous tree; height 5–7 m; mid-green palmate leaves, rose-pink flowers in May and June.

Agapanthus orientalis African lily; half hardy; height 30–40 cm; mid-green leaves, blue or blue-and-white flowers.

Ageratum houstonianum or *A. mexicanum* half-hardy annual; height 12–30 cm; heart-shaped mid-green hairy leaves, large bright blue flowers from early summer.

Anemone hupehensis hardy herbaceous perennial; height 0.75–1 m; wide mauve-pink flowers from August to September.

Artemisia absinthium common wormwood; hardy deciduous shrub; height 1 m; silver-grey leaves, small yellow flowers in July and August.

A. stelleriana dusty miller; hardy perennial; height 40–52 cm; ovate white leaves, panicles of yellow flowers in August and September.

Astilbe × crispa hardy herbaceous perennial; height 15–20 cm; ovate, mid-green slightly crinkled leaves, tiny flowers opening in plumes in July and August.

Aucuba japonica spotted laurel; evergreen shrub; height 2–4 m; dark green leathery leaves, olive green star-shaped flowers in March and April.

Begonia semperflorens fibrous-rooted species; height 15–25 cm; glossy bright green or purple leaves, red, pink or white flowers from June to September.

Bellis perennis daisy; hardy perennial; height 12–15 cm; mid-green leaves, white flowers between March and October.

Bergenia purpurascens hardy evergreen herbaceous perennial; height 40 cm; narrow ovate leaves, bell-shaped purple-pink flowers in April and May.

B. cordifolia hardy evergreen herbaceous perennial; height 30 cm; rounded leaves, bell-shaped lilac flowers in March and April.

Betula albo-sinensis birch tree; height 6–7 m; ovate mid-green leaves, orange-red bark.

B. papyrifera paper birch; height 7–10 cm; triangular mid-green leaves, white bark.

Callicarpa japonica deciduous shrub; height 1.6 m; pale to mid-green ovate slender-pointed leaves, pink flowers in August, lilac-purple berries.

Camellia japonica common camellia; hardy evergreen tree; height 2–4 m; ovate glossy dark green leaves, white, pink or purple flowers between February and May.

Campanula medium Canterbury bell; hardy biennial; height 0.3–1 m; long bright green hairy leaves, white, blue, pink or purple bell-shaped flowers from May to July.

C. portenschlagiana dwarf perennial; height 15 cm; heart-shaped mid-green leaves, deep blue-purple bell-shaped flowers between June and November.

Carpinus betulus common hornbeam; deciduous tree; height 5–8 m; mid-green ovate veined leaves, catkins in April and May.

Catalpa bignonioides Indian bean tree; hardy deciduous tree; height 5–7 m; bright green heart-shaped leaves, white flowers with yellow and purple tinges in July.

Centaurea cyanus cornflower; annual herbaceous plant; height 0.75–1 m; lanceolate grey-green leaves, pink, red, purple, blue or white flowers from June to September.

Cerastium tomentosum snow-in-summer; hardy annual; height 10–15 cm; woolly silver-grey leaves, small white flowers in May and June.

Chamaecyparis obtusa 'Nana Variegata' Hinoki cypress; slow-growing hardy evergreen dwarf coniferous; height 60 cm; dense dark green foliage.

C. pisifera 'Plumosa' Sawara cypress; height 10 m; fluffy pale green foliage.

Choisya ternata evergreen flowering shrub; height, 1.6–2 m; trifoliate glossy green leaves, sweet-scented white flowers in April and May.

Clematis montana deciduous flowering climber; height 12 m; trifoliate dark green leaves, white flowers in July and August.

C. texensis tender deciduous species; height 2–4 m; leaves made up of four to eight ovate leaflets, red flowers from June to September.

Convallaria majalis 'Rosea' lily of the valley; hardy herbaceous perennial; height 15–20 cm; elliptic mid-green leaves, pink flowers in April and May.

Corylus avellana 'Contorta' corkscrew hazel; hardy deciduous nut-bearing tree; height 3 m; mid-green ovate leaves, yellow catkins in February.

C. horizontalis deciduous species; height 15–18 cm; ovate dark green leaves turning red in autumn, pink flowers in June followed by red berries.

Crocus imperati hardy dwarf plant; height 7–10 cm; buff-coloured outer petals, bright purple inner ones.

Daphne cneorum garland flower; evergreen shrub; height 15 cm; narrow oblong leaves, highly scented pink flowers in May and June.

Deutzia gracilis hardy deciduous flowering shrub; height 1–1.2 m; mid-green toothed leaves, white star-shaped flowers in June.

Dicentra eximia hardy herbaceous perennial; height 30–45 cm; grey-green fern-like leaves, bright pink flowers from May to September.

Elaeagnus angustifolia oleaster; deciduous shrub or tree; height 3–5 m;

narrow grey-green leaves, silvery flowers in June followed by edible fruits.

E. pungens 'Aurea' evergreen shrub; height 2.75–4 m; glossy green ovate leaves that are white underneath, silver flowers in October and November.

Eschscholzia californica Californian poppy; height 30–40 cm; blue-green leaves, bright orange-yellow flowers from June to October.

Euonymus fortunei spindle tree; creeping evergreen shrub; height up to 3.5 m against a wall; dark green glossy ovate leaves, small green-white flowers in May and June.

Fagus sylvatica 'Purpurea Pendula' weeping form of common purple beech; purple-red ovate leaves, thick grey trunk.

Fatsia japonica erect evergreen shrub; height 2.5–5 m; mid to deep green palmate leaves, white flowers in October.

Forsythia × intermedia 'Spectabilis' evergreen shrub; height 2.75 m; dark green toothed leaves, bright yellow flowers in March and April.

Fuchsia fulgens tender shrub; height 1–1.5 m; pale to mid-green ovate or heart-shaped leaves, scarlet flowers tipped with green between July and October.

Gleditsia triacanthos 'Sunburst' honey locust; hardy deciduous tree; height 6–10 m; golden-yellow pinnate leaves.

Gypsophila repens hardy alpine species; height 15 cm; grey-green leaves, white to deep pink flowers between June and August.

Helleborus orientalis lenten rose; hardy perennial; height 45–60 cm; broad dark green leaves, cream flowers in February and March.

Helxine soleirolii mind your own business; creeping half-hardy perennial; rounded pale to mid-green leaves.

Hosta lancifolia hardy herbaceous perennial; height 60 cm; glossy narrow mid-green leaves, lilac flowers from July to September.

H. plantaginea hardy herbaceous perennial; height 45–60 cm; heart-shaped yellow-green leaves, white flowers in August and September.

Iberis saxatilis candytuft; hardy alpine species; height 7 cm; dark green leaves, white flowers from May to July.

Iris fulva beardless iris; height 45 cm; flat, slender evergreen leaves, terracotta flowers in mid-June.

I. susiana mourning iris; bearded; height 45 cm; sickle-shaped leaves, pale grey flowers with purple veins in May or June.

Jasminum nudiflorum winter-flowering jasmine; hardy deciduous shrub; height 3 m; smooth dark green trifoliate leaves, bright yellow flowers from November to April.

J. × stephanense hybrid climber; height 3–5 m; dull green leaves with five leaflets, pale pink flowers in June.

Lamium galeobdolon 'variegatum' yellow archangel; hardy perennial; height 15–45 cm; silver-green leaves, yellow flowers in June and July.

Lantana camara evergreen shrub; height 0.4–1.2 m; mid to deep green elliptic leaves, white, yellow or red flowers from May to October.

Laurus nobilis sweet bay; hardy evergreen shrub; height 3–6 m; mid to dark green glossy lanceolate leaves, yellow-green flowers in April.

Lilium regale hardy stem-rooting lily; height 1–2 m; fragrant white flowers with dark pink backs and bright yellow centres in July.

L. rubellum stem-rooting lily; height 30–75 cm; rose-pink bell-shaped flowers in May and June.

Linum grandiflorum 'Rubrum' scarlet flax; hardy annual; height 30 cm; narrow pale green leaves, crimson flowers from June to August.

Lobelia erinus half-hardy perennial; height 10–25 cm; light green ovate leaves, pale blue and white flowers from May.

Magnolia grandiflora hardy evergreen tree; height 3–5 m; dark green glossy ovate leaves, cream-white flowers between July and September.

M. stellata slow-growing deciduous tree; height 2.75–4 m; pale green lanceolate leaves, white star-shaped flowers in March and April.

Mahonia aquifolium Oregon grape; hardy evergreen shrub; height 1–1.75 m; dark green glossy leaves, deep yellow flowers in March and April.

M. japonica height 2.75–3.2 m; dark green pinnate leaves, lemon yellow flowers between January and March.

Malus hupehensis crab apple; height 8–10 m; deep green serrated leaves, white flowers tipped with pink in May and June, red-tinged yellow fruit.

Narcissus triandrus 'Alba' height 20–40 cm; linear leaves, cream-white back-swept petals.

Nicotiana alata tobacco plant; half-hardy perennial; height 0.6–1 m; mid-green oblong leaves, white flowers from June to September.

Nigella damascena love-in-a-mist; hardy annual; height 60 cm; bright green leaves, blue or white flowers from June to August.

Osmanthus delavayi evergreen flowering shrub; height 2–2.6 m; dark green glossy toothed leaves, white flowers in April.

O. heterophyllus height 2–3.3 m; mid-green leaves, white flowers in September and October.

Osmarea burkwoodii evergreen flowering shrub; height 2–3.3 m; mid-green glossy pointed leaves, white flowers in April and May.

Osmunda regalis flowering fern; height 1.30–1.6 m; lanceolate and bipinnate light green fronds.

Paeonia officinalis herbaceous perennial; height 60 cm; deeply cut mid-green leaves, crimson flowers in May and June.

Parthenocissus tricuspidata hardy deciduous climber; height up to 20 m; three-lobed leaves, yellow-green flowers in June and July.

P. quinquefolia true Virginia creeper; hardy self-clinging species; height up to 25 m; leaves turn brilliant crimson in autumn, green-yellow flowers in May and June followed by blue-black berries.

Passiflora caerulea evergreen flowering climber; height 6–10 m; light to mid-green palmate leaves, white flowers tinged with pink from June to October.

Paulownia tomentosa hardy deciduous flowering tree; height 5–8 m; mid-green heart-shaped leaves open after fragrant lavender-blue flowers.

Philadelphus coronarius hardy deciduous flowering shrub; height 2–3 m; mid-green ovate leaves, white cup-shaped flowers in June and July.

Phyllitis scolopendrium hart's tongue; evergreen fern; height 30–60 cm; bright green strap-shaped fronds.

Picea pungens 'Glauca' Colorado spruce; hardy evergreen coniferous tree; height 7–8 m; stiff grey-blue to blue-green needles, cones borne after about 20 years.

Pieris japonica hardy evergreen flowering shrub; height 2–3 m; oblong leaves turn from copper-red to mid-green, white flowers in March and April.

Platycerium bifurcatum staghorn fern; evergreen; height 0.5–1 m; mid-green round wavy-edged fronds.

Reseda odorata hardy annual; height 30–70 cm; mid-green spatulate leaves, yellow-white flowers from June to October.

Rhododendron catawbiense evergreen shrub; height 2–3 m; dark green oblong shiny leaves, lilac flowers in May and June.

R. indicum evergreen shrub; height 1–2 m; dark green glossy bristly leaves, bright red or pink flowers in June.

R. sutchuenense evergreen tree; height up to 4 m; deep green ovate leaves, rose-lilac flowers in March.

R. williamsianum evergreen shrub; height 1–2m; dark-green kidney-shaped leaves, pink bell-shaped flowers in April.

R. yakushimanum evergreen shrub; height 60 cm; dark green leathery leaves, white bell-shaped flowers in May and June.

Robinia pseudoacacia common or false acacia; hardy deciduous flowering tree; height 10 m; light green ovate leaves, cream-white flowers in June.

Salix alba 'Tristis' hardy deciduous tree; height 7–8 m; pale to mid-green leaves, yellow catkins in March and April.

Santolina chamaecyparissus evergreen dwarf shrub; height 45–60 cm; silvery leaves, lemon-yellow flowers in July.

Sedum acre biting stonecrop; evergreen alpine succulent; height 2.5–5 cm; mid to yellow-green leaves, yellow flowers in June and July.

Skimmia japonica hardy evergreen shrub; height 1–1.75 m; pale green leathery leaves, cream-white flowers followed by red berries in August and September.

Sternbergia lutea hardy bulbous plant; height 10–15 cm; bright yellow flowers in September and October.

Syringa vulgaris common lilac; hardy deciduous tree; height 3–4 m; heart-shaped leaves, lilac-coloured flowers in May and June.

Taxus baccata 'Fastigiata' Irish yew; height 5 m; female form with dark green leaves.

Thuja occidentalis white cedar; height 8 m; flat, dull green leaves that are yellow underneath, yellow cones.

Tilia platyphyllos broad-leaved lime; height 5–6 m; pale broad leaves, yellow-white flowers in June and July.

Tulipa clusiana lady tulip; height 22–30 cm; erect narrow grey-green leaves, white flowers flushed with red in April.

Viburnum carlesii deciduous shrub; height 1.3–1.6 m; dull green ovate leaves, fragrant white flowers in April and May.

V. davidii evergreen species; height 0.6–1 m; ovate veined dark green leaves, white flowers in June, followed by blue berries if male and female forms planted together.

V. rhytidophyllum evergreen species; height 3.3–5 m; glossy dark green leaves, white flowers in May and June, red berries turning black.

Vinca major 'Elegantissima' greater periwinkle; height 15–30 cm; pale green and white leaves, purple-blue flowers between April and June.

V. minor lesser periwinkle; height 5–10 cm; glossy dark green lanceolate leaves, blue flowers between March and July.

Viola cornuta pansy; height 10–30 cm; mid-green oval leaves, lavender flowers in June and July.

V. × wittrockiana garden pansy; height 15–25 cm; mid-green ovate leaves, large flowers ranging in colour from cream to purple between May and September.

Wisteria floribunda 'Longissima Alba' hardy deciduous climbing shrub; height 10 m; mid-green pinnate leaves, long white flowers in May and June.

W. sinensis Chinese wisteria; height up to 30 m; dark green leaves, mauve flowers in May and June.

Zinnia angustifolia half-hardy annual; height 60–70 cm; light green hairy leaves, bright orange flowers from July to August.

INDEX